A 21ST-CENTURY APPROACH TO
School Librarian Evaluation

Related Publications:

Learning4Life (L4L): A National Plan for Implementation of
Standards for the 21st-Century Learner and
Empowering Learners: Guidelines for School Library Programs
Available for download at www.ala.org/aasl/learning4life.

Standards for the 21st-Century Learner (2007)
Available for download from the AASL Web site.
Packets of full-color brochures may be purchased.
Visit www.ala.org/aasl/standards.

 Standards for the 21st-Century Learner in Action (2009)
Available for purchase at www.ala.org/aasl/standardsinaction.

Empowering Learners: Guidelines for School Library Programs (2009)
Available for purchase at www.ala.org/aasl/guidelines.

A Planning Guide for Empowering Learners
with School Library Program Assessment Rubric (2010)
Available for purchase at www.aasl.eb.com, or for more
information and resources visit www.ala.org/aasl/planningguide.

ISBN: 978-0-8389-8618-9

Published by:
American Association of School Librarians
a division of the American Library Association
50 E. Huron St.
Chicago, Illinois 60611-2795

To order, call 800-545-2433, press 7
www.alastore.ala.org/aasl

Cover graphic designed by Louis Henry Mitchell.

A 21st-Century Approach to School Librarian Evaluation, a school librarian evaluation workbook and rubric based on *Empowering Learners: Guidelines for School Library Programs* (2009) and its companion, *A Planning Guide for Empowering Learners with School Library Program Assessment Rubric* (2010), is designed to guide you through the annual professional evaluation process facing every school librarian. The workbook includes multiple sections. The "Take Action" section lists best practices that reflect the duties and responsibilities expected of an exemplary school librarian. The "Evidence of Accomplishment" chart proposes examples of your practice that support the concept of evidence-based performance to be shared during the evaluation process. "Suggested Readings" is a collection of research-based literature citations assembled around the best practices of school librarianship.

Also included in the workbook is a school librarian evaluation rubric based on the guidelines and actions in *Empowering Learners*. Use this rubric to focus your thinking on the conversation you need to have with your administrators before you begin the annual evaluation process. The school librarian evaluation rubric can become your employee evaluation tool or the launching point for creating a personalized tool that is a perfect fit for you and your school.

The end result will be a school librarian evaluation process that guides and supports professional development throughout your career. Interweaving *A 21st-Century Approach to School Librarian Evaluation* with AASL's *A Planning Guide for Empowering Learners* strengthens both evaluation instruments, improves the learning of your students, and meets the needs of all your library stakeholders.

Implementation of the practices advocated in this book are supported by the Learning4Life (L4L) resources: an implementation plan created to support states, school systems, and individual schools preparing to implement the American Association of School Librarians (AASL) learning standards and program guidelines (see <www.ala.org/aasl/guidelinesandstandards/learning4life>).

A 21st-Century Approach to School Librarian Evaluation

ACKNOWLEDGEMENTS

AASL gratefully acknowledges the following:

Written, researched, and edited by:

Patricia Owen

District Information Resource Coordinator/Librarian

Eastwood Local Schools, Ohio

<pattiolibrarian@gmail.com>

AASL Staff Liaison: Stephanie Book

TABLE OF CONTENTS

PREFACE

Following the 2009 publication of *Empowering Learners: Guidelines for School Library Programs*, the American Association of School Librarians (AASL) developed a tool that supports the assessment, planning, and implementation of the national guidelines and helps school librarians advocate for their programs. This tool, *A Planning Guide for Empowering Learners with School Library Program Assessment Rubric*, is designed to ensure that as program planners, school librarians know how to develop goals, effectively apply criteria and utilize accepted principles to build effective school library programs.

While *Empowering Learners* established a new direction for school library programs, its creators also recognized that each program will be different because each must be developed to anticipate and meet the needs of the local school (2009, 11). To ensure that this was achieved, in *A Planning Guide for Empowering Learners* both the program planning guide and assessment rubric build upon the same inquiry-learning approach that served as the foundation for AASL's *Standards for the 21st-Century Learner* and its companion piece, *Standards for the 21st-Century Learner in Action*.

Now, school librarians who implemented the *Empowering Learners* guidelines into their library program planning process can expand on that effort through the use of a new tool for evaluating school librarians that continues the AASL support effort begun with the publication of *Standards for the 21st-Century Learner*.

AASL's new *A 21st-Century Approach to School Librarian Evaluation*, in conjunction with the accompanying "School Librarian Evaluation Rubric," provides a process for school librarians to be evaluated by their administrators using standards that underpin school librarianship and match the unique educational roles performed by school librarians.

Armed with these AASL tools, school librarians can chart their course to plan, design and deliver student instruction, administer and evaluate their library programs, and undergo a meaningful personnel evaluation process that ties the standards and guidelines together in a relevant way.

Susan Ballard
AASL President, 2012–2013

INTRODUCTION

A Brief History

The goal of *A 21st-Century Approach to School Librarian Evaluation* is to help you create an annual professional school librarian evaluation process that is effective for both you and your administrator. The process described in this workbook shares attributes common to many school personnel performance assessments, but it also contains unique features that will support your professional growth, strengthen your school library program, fulfill the needs of your stakeholders, and improve the learning of your students.

Before reading this publication, you'll need to examine the four earlier AASL publications that form the basis for *A 21st-Century Approach to School Librarian Evaluation*.

First, *Standards for the 21st-Century Learner* expands the definition of information literacy to include multiple literacies and introduces overarching learning standards that support global instructional perspectives:

1. Inquire, think critically, and gain knowledge.
2. Draw conclusions, make informed decisions, apply knowledge to new situations, and create new knowledge.
3. Share knowledge and participate ethically and productively as members of our democratic society.
4. Pursue personal and aesthetic growth. (AASL 2007, 3)

Second, *Standards for the 21st-Century Learner in Action* "presents action examples for putting the Standards into practice; the action examples are divided into grade-level sections by benchmark…[and are] designed to give a picture of how a lesson or unit might be designed to teach specific skills, dispositions, responsibilities, and self-assessment strategies" that librarians face in their school libraries (AASL 2009, 10).

Both *Standards for the 21st-Century Learner* and *Standards for the 21st-Century Learner in Action* reveal a number of best practices and beliefs:

- Students need the right climate to be skillful consumers and producers of information.
- Teaching in isolation is ineffective, and collaborative instruction is the goal.
- Students need to be actively engaged in learning.
- School librarians perform five roles (information specialist, teacher, instructional partner, program administrator, and leader) in order to accomplish the school library's mission.
- The school library is both virtual and physical space.
- Student achievement is best accomplished through collaborative efforts of all the school stakeholders and the school librarian provides the leadership. (AASL 2010, 10)

Third, *Empowering Learners: Guidelines for School Library Programs* "establishes a new direction for library programs. It also recognizes that each library program will be different because each must be developed to anticipate and meet the needs of the local school" (AASL 2010, 11).

Fourth, *A Planning Guide for Empowering Learners with School Library Program Assessment Rubric* provides an evaluation tool to measure programmatic progress. "The planning process will determine the goals and objectives of the program, strategies to reach these goals, and the resources...that are needed to implement the program" (AASL 2010, 11). The process of developing a school library program is collaborative, involving all library stakeholders, and the *School Library Program Assessment Rubric* is the best tool to drive collaborative programming development. Of course, the school librarian is the primary change agent and provides the leadership for implementation at every step (AASL 2010, 11).

Changing Educational Scene

Now is the opportune time to develop new approaches for school librarian evaluation. Following the launching of President Obama's Race to the Top (RTTT) initiative in 2009, school district funding applications now require compliance with several educational policies. As a result, any proposal for the creation of an assessment tool to evaluate school district personnel must entail a host of new components: (1) Common Core Standards adoption, (2) measuring evidence of student learning, (3) merit pay compensation, (4) evidence-based data collection, (5) value-added modeling, (6) pathway provisions for aspiring teachers and principals, (7) closing the gap between low- and high-achieving school districts, (8) transitioning to common assessments and (9) technology commitment (U.S. Dept. of Ed. 2009).

Perhaps the most important of the new components is the *Common Core State Standards.* The Common Core State Standards Initiative (2009–2010), led by members of the National Governors Association Center for Best Practices and the Council of Chief State School Officers, was a collaboration of representatives of K–12 teachers, school administrators, and educational researchers. Feedback on the standards came from stakeholders including higher education representatives, educational-policy makers, school administrators, content experts, civil rights organizations, student advocate associations, business people, English language learning experts, challenged students, parents, and the public.

The end product, the *Common Core State Standards*, describes what K–12 students should learn and what high school students should know to be college- and career-ready by the time they graduate. Individual states have the responsibility to implement the standards and use them to measure the growth of their students (Common Core State Standards Initiative 2011a, 2011b).

As states begin adopting all or portions of these standards, much of the traditional stand-alone school library information literacy curriculum is being incorporated into core areas of the school instructional program. From now on, school librarians are expected to collaborate with classroom and support staff teachers to deliver instruction, and these partnerships will now receive support at national, state, and local school administration levels.

Also, according to *Empowering Learners: Guidelines for School Library Programs,* school librarians must, "recognize and connect the new learning standards and guidelines to content area curriculum standards, resulting in improved teaching and learning" (AASL 2009, 6), and collaborate "with educators and students to design and teach engaging learning experiences" (AASL 2009, 8). Focusing on the learning process, not on the more limited concept of information literacy is also embraced by *Standards for the 21st-Century Learner* (AASL 2009, 12). In short, the current AASL position on the roles of school librarians places the school librarian in the school community as a collaborative teacher, not a lone instructor.

Library best practices also reinforce the position that the most effective way to impact student learning is through collaborative classroom lessons, co-planned, co-taught, and co-assessed with fellow teachers. "The teaching of 21st-century skills requires that all aspects of teaching and learning are built on collaborative partnerships....These collaborative partnerships require creativity, an openness to trying new approaches, and a willingness to take risks.... All members of the learning community now share the roles of teacher, learner, and collaborative partner.... By modeling such collaborative relationships, the school librarian helps change the culture of the learning community to reflect the kind of relationships that comprise the 21st-century work environment" (AASL 2009, 20–21).

And so, recent changes in the national educational landscape (RTTT, state adoption of Common Core State Standards, and collaborative teaching) must be incorporated into the way school librarians teach. Accordingly, school librarians will be evaluated on collaborative lessons, co-planned, co-taught, and co-assessed with their colleagues in the classroom or library, wherever instruction takes place. Because the teaching role of school librarians has changed, so, too, must their evaluation tools. This book provides the framework for school librarians to align their evaluation process with national initiatives as well as the professional standards expressed in *Empowering Learners.* School librarians who use the process described here will be well prepared to face their annual performance evaluation with confidence.

PREPARING FOR THE EVALUATION PROCESS

What is your personal vision of the ideal school librarian evaluation process? Before you describe your vision and begin the process of creating the tools that will make the process a reality, think about your past performance evaluation experiences. Consider evaluation experiences that led you forward in your career. What about those experiences propelled you to develop as a school librarian? Were the expectations clearly defined? Did the evaluation include detailed descriptions of how to improve and grow? Were you a collaborator in the evaluation process? Next, recall any negative aspects of your evaluation experiences. What made those experiences less helpful? Make a list of these experiences and refer to it as you participate in the process of creating your own evaluation tools.

A New Approach to School Librarian Evaluation

This book provides a system for evaluating school librarians that can be used "as is" or as a foundation for creating a personalized evaluation form that reflects your school district's unique needs. Working in conjunction with your principal, you can use *A 21st-Century Approach to School Librarian Evaluation* as a basis for collaborative conversations to determine the form your school adopts.

The Benefits of School Librarian Evaluation

With the program guidelines outlined in *Empowering Learners* as a backdrop, the process of creating librarian-evaluation forms and rubrics in tandem with your administrator provides multiple benefits to all participants:

1. The process is a self-reflective experience that offers a rare chance to assess your own professional learning.

2. The process provides an opportunity to design an evaluation tool. Oftentimes, classroom teachers and other school personnel are evaluated with forms that were developed without their input. School librarians using *A 21st-Century Approach to School Librarian Evaluation* have the chance to significantly impact the tools used to evaluate them.

3. Because you take part in tailoring the tool, you can use it to educate others about what school librarians do; this education is a critical component of school library advocacy.

4. By demonstrating leadership in the process of creating your evaluation tool, you can also establish an assessment leadership role in your school district.

5. Creating an evaluation tool in partnership with your principal is a collaborative opportunity to share measurable, evidence-based practices that you employ every day; it's also a chance to raise the awareness of all your stakeholders about your performance. Providing the principal with an evaluation tool that both matches the unique duties and responsibilities of the library position, and informs administrators about the significant impact of librarians on student learning is one of the great benefits of creating your own tool based on AASL's program guidelines.

6. The school librarian evaluation form you create will look like classroom teacher evaluation forms that are easily recognizable by principals, boards of educations, and teacher unions.

7. Another benefit is that the new form you create, using this workbook and rubric, can accommodate the ongoing changes occurring in the educational profession in the wake of the RTTT funding initiative and state adoption of nationally developed standards.

Personnel Evaluation and Program Evaluation Are Not the Same

This publication is based on the program guidelines found in *Empowering Learners: Guidelines for School Library Programs* and *A Planning Guide for Empowering Learners with School Library Program Assessment Rubric*. While these earlier publications share the same foundation as this workbook, they address different needs. The program publications guide development and assessment of school library programs; however, this workbook is a framework for evaluating school librarians.

In many ways, evaluating a program and evaluating personnel are very different; the two tasks are not equivalent, nor interchangeable. Program assessment seeks to examine strengths and weaknesses of an entire school library program; that task is the province of a team of school stakeholders. Evaluation of a school librarian involves analysis of individual job performance and employee accountability. In contrast to program assessment, personnel evaluation may result in the awarding of tenure or other contractual changes, and laws and regulations affecting boards of education and teachers' unions come into play (Owen 2011, 32–33). Although the AASL tools are somewhat different, they are complementary, and school librarians should use them together.

How to Use the Workbook

A 21st-Century Approach to School Librarian Evaluation is formatted as a workbook and consists of multiple elements under each guideline and action including: Suggested Readings, Take Action, Collect Evidence, and My Action Plan. The workbook content is based on the program guidelines found in *Empowering Learners* which serves as the structure for the school librarian evaluation rubric. The main body of the workbook mirrors the guidelines and is divided into three parts:

– Teaching for Learning, Guidelines 1 through 5

– Building the Learning Environment, Guidelines 6 through 13

– Empowering Learning through Leadership, Guideline 14

The *Teaching for Learning* section includes school librarian actions in the areas of collaboration, reading skills, multiple literacies instruction, inquiry-based research and instruction, and assessment of student learning. The actions appear in the workbook under the headings below.

1.1 Building Collaborative Partnerships

1.2 The Role of Reading

1.3 Addressing Multiple Literacies

1.4 Effective Practices for Inquiry

1.5 Assessment in Teaching for Learning

The *Building the Learning Environment* section focuses on strategic planning, staffing, space and resources, funding, ethics and equal access, collection development, advocacy, and professional development. The actions appear in the workbook under the headings below.

2.1 Planning and Evaluating

2.2 Staffing

2.3 Learning Space

2.4 Budget

2.5 Policies

2.6 Collection and Information Access

2.7 Outreach

2.8 Professional Development

The *Empowering Learning through Leadership* section focuses on leadership and best practices. The actions appear in the workbook under the heading below.

3.1 Leadership and Best Practices

Each section of this workbook begins with an *Empowering Learners* program guideline recast as a school librarian evaluation guideline. For example, 1.1 "promotes collaboration among members of the learning community and encourages learners to be independent, lifelong users and produces of ideas and information" is based on a program guideline in *Empowering Learners* (AASL 2009, 20). Under the 1.1 guideline is a list of "Suggested Readings" that highlight best practices found in library literature. Additional readings are included in an appendix.

Following the 1.1 guideline page is a section labeled "Take Action" which lists the actions found under that guideline, for example: 1.1.a "collaborates with a core team of classroom teachers and specialists to design, implement, and evaluate inquiry lessons and units" (AASL 2009, 20). Below each action are tips or strategies and techniques to help you brainstorm future actions and decisions.

On the next worksheet page, "Collect Evidence", school librarians can enter examples of evidence. An appendix with dozens of evidence examples is provided at the end of the workbook.

Last, a "My Action Plan" worksheet is provided. Librarians can use this worksheet to enter information in spaces labeled My Notes, My Goals, My Target Audience, My Tasks and Timeline, and My Professional Development. Action plans can be expanded by copying worksheets for multiple actions or goals, and by using the enlarged "My Action Plan Template" in Appendix F 146.

Detailed directions for using the worksheets are at the top of each page, but librarians can adapt them to meet their professional needs. Librarians who proceed step-by-step through *A 21st-Century Approach to School Librarian Evaluation* will emerge prepared for their annual performance evaluation.

How to Use the Rubric

Like rubrics used to assess student learning, the full-model rubric in Appendix A is formatted on a series of grids. Each grid is headlined by one of 14 criteria. These criteria are derived from the *Empowering Learners* guidelines and state the essential characteristics of school library programs. For each guideline, actions or tasks of successful school librarians are grouped under four performance levels displayed across the top of the grid: Foundational, Developing, Mastery, and Exemplary.

In the cells below the performance levels (columns), performance descriptions are provided. These descriptions are based on the actions listed under the guidelines in *Empowering Learners*. At all levels, the performance descriptions provide detailed indications of school librarian accomplishments. These descriptions clearly state what each level (Foundational, Developing, Mastery and Exemplary) of school librarian actions "look like." By articulating specific actions clearly, performance descriptions decrease subjectivity in evaluation. Because the actions that make up the descriptions are embedded in professional guidelines, they are credible.

The performance descriptions are distributed across four levels based on degrees of developmental complexity. Actions listed at the "Foundational" level might be expected of first-year school librarians. In contrast, actions listed at the "Exemplary" level represent high levels of expertise and, often, the culmination of many years of work, planning, and effort. Performing all the "Exemplary" actions may not be achieved until a school librarian is a veteran. The middle-level descriptions describe typical milestones along the continuum of school librarian development. When viewed in the context of multiple levels, performance descriptions also establish expectations, provide benchmarks attainable over time, and facilitate the identification of "stretch goals" that may take time and effort to achieve.

The full-model rubric may be used in its current form or adapted by librarians to fit specific needs. It's designed to be shared with administrators as part of pre-evaluation conversations.

In addition to the full-model rubric described above, an additional summative rubric format is included in this book. Summative forms are used by the principal as a final evaluation tool; they are placed in the personnel file at the end of the year. School librarians can also choose to adapt the full-model rubric by isolating one performance level and converting it into a checklist or goal list to guide their practice.

Gathering Evidence and Building an Evaluation Portfolio

This book contains dozens of evidence suggestions to support your accomplishments in Appendix C at the end of the workbook.

Evidence-gathering is an ongoing process and needs to be organized into a print or electronic portfolio (e.g., 3-ring binder, website, or learning management system). Use the guidelines and actions in the rubric as the structure. Date the evidence and write the matching guideline or action on each piece of evidence. Every event, lesson, committee meeting, teaching strategy, student product, facility change, agenda, website update, assessment, thank-you letter, promotion, and teaching tool is a potential piece of measurable and objective evidence to add to your portfolio. Consider working with a colleague. Use a calendar reminder to update the portfolio periodically.

Conversing With Administrators

Take your evidence portfolio to your pre-observation, formal observation, and post-observation librarian evaluation meetings; it is an organized documentation of your performance. The evidence portfolio provides a structure to make sure your evaluation will be based on measureable, objective, evidence-based practices.

Work with your principal to agree upon a specific guideline(s) to focus on during the next evaluation period and use both the evaluation portfolio and this workbook to set future goals. Allow the portfolio to turn your evaluation conversation into a launch pad for school library advocacy.

EVALUATION WORKBOOK

1.1 TEACHING FOR LEARNING:
Building Collaborative Partnerships

Guideline

promotes collaboration among members of the learning community and encourages learners to be independent, lifelong users and producers of ideas and information

SUGGESTED READINGS

Examine these readings to learn best practices for achieving this guideline. As you read, look for new strategies to expand your professional practice and use the "My Notes" space to record your ideas.

Alexander, L. B., R. C. Smith, and J. O. Carey. 2003 . "Education Reform and the School Library Media Specialist: Perceptions of Principals." *Knowledge Quest* 32 (2): 10–13.

American Association of School Librarians. 2012. "Essential Links: Resources for Library Program Development: Common Core State Standards." <http://aasl.ala.org/essentiallinks/index.php?title=Common_Core_State_Standards> (accessed March 18, 2012).

Carr, J., and I. F. Rockman. 2003. "Information-Literacy Collaboration: A Shared Responsibility." *American Libraries* 34 (8): 52–54.

Coatney, S. 2005. "Testing, Testing, Testing." *Teacher Librarian* 32 (5): 50.

Davies, A. 2001. "Involving Students in Communicating about Their Learning." *NASSP Bulletin* 85 (621): 47–52. <http://annedavies.com/images/PDFs/involving_students.pdf> (accessed March 11, 2012).

Dinges, C., and M. Ginnane. 2009. "The Owl and the Pussy-Cat Go to Sea: A Cross-Organizational Conversation." *OLA Quarterly* 15 (4): 30–32.

Hartzell, G. 2003. "Why Should Principals Support School Libraries?" *Teacher Librarian* 31 (2): 21–23.

Kuhlthau, C. C., L. K. Maniotes, and A. K. Caspari. 2012. *Guided Inquiry Design: A Framework for Inquiry in Your School.* Santa Barbara, CA: Libraries Unlimited.

Lau, D. 2002. "Got Clout?" *School Library Journal* 48 (5): 40–45.

Loertscher, D. V., C. Koechlin, and S. Zwaan. 2011. *Beyond Bird Units: Thinking and Understanding in Information-Rich and Technology-Rich Environments.* Salt Lake City, UT: Hi Willow Research & Publishing.

Mann, S. 2011. "21st-Century School Librarians: Envisioning the Future." *School Library Monthly* 28 (2): 29–30.

CONTINUED ON PAGE 131

My Notes

TAKE ACTION

Use these "Take Action" tips to help you brainstorm strategies you'll implement in your library program. Record your ideas and plans in the "My Actions" space provided.

Action 1.1.a "Take Action" Tips

collaborates with a core team of classroom teachers and specialists to design, implement, and evaluate inquiry lessons and units

❑ Get on department/team/grade-level meeting agendas (weekly, biweekly, monthly) and join school-wide committees such as technology, professional development, and curriculum.

❑ Attend school activities, such as the science fair, quiz bowl, and drama club, or lead school activities, such as a book club or technology club.

❑ Become an expert on the interdisciplinary features of your state's adopted standards.

❑ Exchange feedback about teaching strategies in a constructive environment to improve student learning.

❑ Use AASL's *A Planning Guide for Empowering Learners* to help you develop and work collaboratively with a school library program planning team that involves a diverse group of stakeholders.

❑ Use the AASL *Standards for the 21st-Century* Learner Lesson Plan Database to search for and develop your own collaborative inquiry lessons aligned with the Common Core State Standards.

❑ Use AASL's Common Core crosswalks to compare standards by grade level.

❑ Use AASL's Common Core crosswalks to align student learning standards with Common Core skills and activities.

❑ Use the power of the Common Core State Standards movement to increase your curriculum leadership role in your school.

❑ Apply for AASL's Collaborative School Library Award to focus attention on a program, unit, or event you planned in collaboration with another educator in your school.

Action 1.1.b "Take Action" Tips

collaborates with an extended team that includes parents, members of the community, museums, academic and public libraries, municipal services, private organizations, and commercial entities to include their expertise and assistance in inquiry lessons and units

❑ Use AASL's *School Library Program Health and Wellness Toolkit* to build stakeholder support and true advocacy for your program.

❑ Join the parent-teacher organization, the Friends group of your public library, local museum groups, and other nonprofit organizations, and include their expertise in your lessons.

❑ Attend Chamber of Commerce meetings and seek out sponsors in the business community.

❑ Employ the advocacy brochures from AASL's *School Libraries Improve Student Learning* series as a tool to help guide discussion with stakeholders in your community: teachers, administrators, parents, and policy-makers.

Action 1.1.c "Take Action" Tips

works with administrators to actively promote, support, and implement collaboration

❑ Initiate collaboration with teachers to create "co-teaching" inquiry lessons and units.

❑ Share the visual action-plan charts and rubric graphs in AASL's *A Planning Guide for Empowering Learners* to help you present snapshot data to your administrators.

❑ Schedule periodic meetings with your principal (at the end of grading periods) and your superintendent (at the end of the semester), and submit periodic reports in multiple formats.

1.1   TEACHING FOR LEARNING: Building Collaborative Partnerships

❑ Invite your principal or assistant principal to serve on your diverse and collaborative school library program planning team.

❑ Get on the school board (board of education) agenda to share student products, program promotions, etc.

❑ Join district-wide committees such as technology, strategic planning, curriculum, school improvement, and RTI (Response to Intervention).

Action 1.1.d "Take Action" Tips

seeks input from students on the learning process

❑ Provide a suggestion box and elicit feedback via a variety of Web 2.0 polling and survey tools.

❑ Consult with students about collection purchases.

❑ Ask students to serve on the library advisory committee or volunteer in the library.

❑ Encourage students to help create assessment tools.

❑ Place students in charge of soliciting displays of student work in all areas of the curriculum.

❑ Collect student input via student response systems (SRS) or cell-phone polls during lessons.

❑ Form student panels and pose questions to them on how they feel about classroom learning strategies.

❑ Arrange for students to communicate their work to an audience of parents and school staff.

My Actions

_____

_____

_____

_____

_____

_____

_____

_____

_____

_____

_____

_____

_____

_____

_____

_____

_____

_____

_____

_____

_____

_____

_____

COLLECT EVIDENCE

Multiple examples of "Evidence of Accomplishment" are located in the Appendix at the end of this workbook. Review the list of potential evidence and select items that document the work you already do in your library. Brainstorm ways that you can add new evidence to your practice. Enter the action you will be implementing below. Use the "My Evidence of Accomplishment" space to record and organize evidence of your practice that you've already collected or plan to collect. Create a portfolio and share it with your principal during the librarian evaluation process.

ACTION _____

_____

My Evidence of Accomplishment

_____

_____

_____

_____

_____

_____

_____

_____

_____

_____

_____

_____

_____

MY ACTION PLAN KEY:

Goal Type

Short-term
Long-term
Part of Strategic Plan
Professional Development
Leader Role
Instructional Partner Role
Information Specialist Role
Teacher Role
Program Administrator Role

My Target Audience

SCHOOL COMMUNITY:

Students
Teachers
Administrators
Advisory Committee
Planning Committee
Friends of the Library
Volunteers (Student/Adult)

EXTERNAL STAKEHOLDERS:

Parents
Local Community
Business Community
Public Library
Academic Library
State Community
National Community
Global Community

My Professional Development Venue

District In-Service
Local/Regional Conference
State Conference
AASL National Conference
Community Learning
College Course
Evidence Collection
Action Research
Readings

Task Timeline

This Week
This Month
This Grading Period
This Semester
This Year
Next Year
2–3 Year Plan

MY ACTION PLAN

Use the "My Action Plan" worksheet to guide your planning process to accomplish the guideline action. After digesting the readings, noting appropriate action strategies, and entering your evidence information, consider and record your goals, target audience, tasks, timelines, and professional development plans. Enter the action you will be implementing below and use the key in the sidebar to help you complete your plan.

ACTION _____

_____

_____

MY GOAL

	Task 1	Timeline
	Task 2	Timeline
	Task 3	Timeline
Goal Type: _____ My Target Audience: _____		
My Professional Development Plan		Venue

MY GOAL

	Task 1	Timeline
	Task 2	Timeline
	Task 3	Timeline
Goal Type: _____ My Target Audience: _____		
My Professional Development Plan		Venue

MY GOAL

	Task 1	Timeline
	Task 2	Timeline
	Task 3	Timeline
Goal Type: _____ My Target Audience: _____		
My Professional Development Plan		Venue

TEACHING FOR LEARNING:
The Role of Reading

Guideline

promotes reading as a foundational skill for learning, personal growth, and enjoyment

SUGGESTED READINGS

Examine these readings to learn best practices for achieving this guideline. As you read, look for new strategies to expand your professional practice and use the "My Notes" space to record your ideas.

American Association of School Librarians. 2010. *Position Statement on the School Librarian's Role in Reading.* <www.ala.org/aasl/aaslissues/positionstatements/roleinreading> (accessed May 19, 2012).

———. 2012. "Essential Links: Resources for Library Program Development: Literacy." <http://aasl.ala.org/essentiallinks/index.php?title=Literacy> (accessed March 11, 2012).

Barack, L. 2010. "A Kindle Program of Their Own." *School Library Journal* 56 (12): 12.

Buddy, J. W. 2011. "Connecting Males and Reading." *School Library Monthly* 28 (2): 11–13.

Center for the Book. 2010. *Letters about Literature.* <www.lettersaboutliterature.org> (accessed May 19, 2012).

Chance, R., and L. Shenaman. 2012. *Crash Course in Family Literacy Programs.* Santa Barbara, CA: Libraries Unlimited.

Commonwealth of Australia. 2002. "MyRead: Strategies for Teaching Reading in the Middle Years." <www.myread.org/organisation.htm> (accessed May 19, 2012).

Cullinan, B. E. 2000. "Independent Reading and School Achievement." <www.ala.org/aasl/aaslpubsandjournals/slmrb/slmrcontents/volume32000/independent> (accessed May 19, 2012).

Deskins, L. 2011. "Parents, Reading Partners, Library Advocates." *Library Media Connection* 30 (3): 34–35.

Doiron, R. 2003. "Motivating the Lifelong Reading Habit through a Balanced Use of Children's Information Books." *School Libraries Worldwide* 9 (1): 39–49.

Follos, A. M. G. 2006. *Reviving Reading: School Library Programming, Author Visits, and Books That Rock!* Westport, CT: Libraries Unlimited.

CONTINUED ON PAGE 131

TAKE ACTION

Use these "Take Action" tips to help you brainstorm strategies you'll implement in your library program. Record your ideas and plans in the "My Actions" space provided.

Action 1.2.a "Take Action" Tips

acquires and promotes current, high-quality, high-interest collections of books and other reading resources in multiple formats

❑ Share reading recommendations on your OPAC and website with Web 2.0 tools, and add a reading-review system to provide interactivity (e.g., Bookshelf, ChiliFresh).

❑ Conduct promotional events at the local, state, and national levels, as well as participate in summer reading programs in the district and with public libraries.

❑ Research and read literature on collection development, such as AASL's *Collection Development for the School Library Media Program: A Beginner's Guide*.

Action 1.2.b "Take Action" Tips

fosters reading for various pursuits, including personal pleasure, knowledge, and ideas

❑ Invite public and academic librarians to speak with students on a variety of topics.

❑ Encourage school groups, such as the high school astronomy club, to meet in the library, and provide them with appropriate materials to check out.

❑ Encourage teachers to meet in the library to discuss topics such as comparing brands of e-readers.

❑ Form book clubs for various interest groups such as teachers and students, males only, and genre-related.

Action 1.2.c "Take Action" Tips

creates an environment where independent reading is valued, promoted, and encouraged

❑ Supply students with free choices including nonfiction materials in multiple formats, not just fiction.

❑ Visit a variety of libraries to get ideas on floor plans that support the "learning commons" concept.

❑ Peruse library journal articles for ideas to convert your spaces to reading-rich areas that attract students.

❑ Snap photos of students engaged in reading activities, enlarge, and post.

❑ Buy READ Design Studio poster software, and feature students and staff on posters throughout the school.

❑ Organize "Brown Bag" lunch signups periodically in the library reading area with "Bring-A-Book" as the entrance pass.

❑ Push sustained silent reading (SSR) initiatives.

Action 1.2.d "Take Action" Tips

develops initiatives to encourage and engage learners in reading, writing, and listening for understanding and enjoyment

❑ Access AASL's *School Librarian's Role in Reading Toolkit* and exercise your essential and unique position to partner with other educators to elevate reading development.

❑ Purchase and circulate audiobooks, or link your library website to online audiobook services.

❑ Purchase or circulate e-materials for playing/listening on e-readers, MP3 players, and tablets.

❑ Present in-service training to teachers on sources of free e-books, and promote e-books in school and public library catalogs.

❑ Create a "presentation area" in the library space for students to create, practice, and present.

Action 1.2.e "Take Action" Tips

motivates learners to read fiction and nonfiction through reading aloud, booktalking, displays, exposure to authors, and other means

❏ Consider sharing with other libraries the cost of author/speaker visits.

❏ Find out when authors will be in your area and negotiate reduced prices.

❏ Loop book reviews and trailers on your projectors and whiteboards during school hours and other events.

❏ Invite local storytellers and puppet performers to share their expertise with your students.

❏ Reach out to the drama and speech teachers to research plays and practice performances in the library space.

❏ Start an afterschool literature circle.

Action 1.2.f "Take Action" Tips

creates opportunities to involve caregivers, parents, and other family members in reading

❏ Begin communication with the parents of your students by making introductory calls over the course of the school year.

❏ Use AASL's *Parent Advocate Toolkit* to help you gain parent support of your program.

❏ Ask your volunteers to help you organize "Brown Bag" lunches, book clubs, and invite-the-teachers events.

❏ Hold an annual "thanks to the volunteers" event and make sure teachers and students participate.

❏ Sign up for home tutoring if you are appropriately credentialed.

❏ Consult AASL's "30 Days of Activities" calendar for ideas to attract parents to the library during School Library Month.

❏ Hold open houses and host parent-teacher conferences.

❏ Ask for column space in the school newspaper that is sent home with students.

❏ Add library news to school district mailings.

❏ Ask to be included in teachers' newsletters that are sent home to parents.

❏ Ask parents to volunteer to participate in library story hours and other library events.

Action 1.2.g "Take Action" Tips

models reading strategies in formal and informal instruction

❏ Initiate a sustained silent reading initiative such as "Drop Everything and Read" (D.E.A.R.), and include one or all grade levels in your school.

❏ Help teachers identify nonfiction texts in the content areas for students to read.

❏ Use SQR3, K-W-L and other active reading strategies.

❏ Assign reading "roles" in small-group instruction.

❏ Hone your skills in teaching reading in a content area to help boost students' informational reading skills.

❏ Monitor students as they create and maintain permanent displays devoted to reading, such as Predictive Assessment of Reading (PAR) charts.

❏ Provide print and electronic graphic organizers for students (e.g., Kidspiration and Bubbl.us).

❏ Model "think aloud" reading strategies for students; don't just "tell."

❏ Use the strategy Read-Write-Pair-Share to boost students' reading skills.

❏ Develop a professional reading-strategies library collection for teachers.

❏ Co-plan and co-teach to help students read better in the content areas.

❏ Teach students how to use an electronic auto-summarizing tool to shorten reading passages and boost comprehension.

1.2 TEACHING FOR LEARNING: The Role of Reading

Action 1.2.h "Take Action" Tips

collaborates with teachers and other specialists to integrate reading strategies into lessons and units of instruction

❏ Use AASL's *Standards for the 21st-Century* Learner Lesson Plan Database to work collaboratively with teachers in your school to develop lesson plans that integrate reading strategies and align with Common Core State Standards.

❏ Revisit learning/reviewing reading strategies for your grade levels and curriculum.

❏ Include brainstorming and other prereading activities in your collaborative lessons.

❏ Research how reading strategies help students understand database-retrieved articles.

❏ Preread and prepare with your students in advance of guest speakers and authors.

❏ Survey students to identify the learning strategies that work best for them.

❏ Teach strategies by reading aloud and modeling rereading for comprehension of difficult passages.

❏ Include statements in lessons that generate student responses of wonder or shock.

❏ Encourage teachers to store practice materials such as vocabulary flashcards in the library for further student review.

❏ Prepare a file of Common Core State Standards "exemplars" for teachers to use.

My Actions

_____

_____

_____

_____

_____

_____

_____

_____

_____

_____

_____

_____

_____

_____

_____

_____

_____

_____

_____

_____

_____

_____

COLLECT EVIDENCE

Multiple examples of "Evidence of Accomplishment" are located in the Appendix at the end of this workbook. Review the list of potential evidence and select items that document the work you already do in your library. Brainstorm ways that you can add new evidence to your practice. Enter the action you will be implementing below. Use the "My Evidence of Accomplishment" space to record and organize evidence of your practice that you've already collected or plan to collect. Create a portfolio and share it with your principal during the librarian evaluation process.

ACTION _____

_____

_____

My Evidence of Accomplishment

MY ACTION PLAN

Use the "My Action Plan" worksheet to guide your planning process to accomplish the guideline action. After digesting the readings, noting appropriate action strategies, and entering your evidence information, consider and record your goals, target audience, tasks, timelines, and professional development plans. Enter the action you will be implementing below and use the key in the sidebar to help you complete your plan.

ACTION _____

_____ _____

_____

MY GOAL

	Task 1	Timeline
	Task 2	Timeline
Goal Type: _____ My Target Audience: _____	Task 3	Timeline

My Professional Development Plan	Venue

MY GOAL

	Task 1	Timeline
	Task 2	Timeline
Goal Type: _____ My Target Audience: _____	Task 3	Timeline

My Professional Development Plan	Venue

MY GOAL

	Task 1	Timeline
	Task 2	Timeline
Goal Type: _____ My Target Audience: _____	Task 3	Timeline

My Professional Development Plan	Venue

TEACHING FOR LEARNING:
Addressing Multiple Literacies

Guideline

provides instruction that addresses multiple literacies, including information literacy, media literacy, visual literacy, and technology literacy

SUGGESTED READINGS

Examine these readings to learn best practices for achieving this guideline. As you read, look for new strategies to expand your professional practice and use the "My Notes" space to record your ideas.

American Association of School Librarians, SLMS Role In Reading Task Force. 2009. "What Every Teacher Should Know about Teaching Multiple Literacies Strategies." <www.ala.org/aasl/sites/ala.org.aasl/files/content/aaslissues/toolkits/slroleinreading/rrtfmultipleliteracies.ppt> (accessed March 10, 2012).

Arnone, M. P. 2010. "How Do School Librarians Perceive Disposition for Learning and Social Responsibility?" *School Library Monthly* 26 (7): 40–43

Burt, D. 2012. "Public Domain eBooks." *School Library Monthly* 28 (5): 40–41.

Callison, D. 1999. "Synthesis: Cognitive Process of Synthesizing Information." *School Library Media Activities Monthly* 15 (10): 39–41, 46.

Callison, D., and A. Lamb. 2004. "Authentic Learning." *School Library Media Activities Monthly* 21 (4): 34–39.

Champlin, C., N. A. Miller, and D. V. Loertscher. 2009. *A Painless Guide to Research Using Web 2.0 Tools.* Salt Lake City: Hi Willow Research & Publishing.

Elder, L. 2003. *Teacher's Manual: The Miniature Guide to Critical Thinking for Children.* Tomales, CA: Foundation for Critical Thinking. <www.criticalthinking.org/store/products/teachers-manual-for-540m-childrens-mini-guide/186> (accessed March 11, 2012).

Everhart, N., and J. Dutilloy. 2003. "Combating Plagiarism: The Role of the School Library Media Specialist." *Knowledge Quest* 31 (4): 43–45.

Fredrick, K. 2010. "In the Driver's Seat: Learning and Library 2.0 Tools." *School Library Monthly* 26 (6): 34–35.

Fredrick, K. 2012. "Sharing Your Library with Facebook Pages." *School Library Monthly* 28 (5): 24–26.

My Notes

CONTINUED ON PAGE 132

TAKE ACTION

Use these "Take Action" tips to help you brainstorm strategies you'll implement in your library program. Record your ideas and plans in the "My Actions" space provided.

Action 1.3.a "Take Action" Tips

promotes critical thinking by connecting learners with the world of information in multiple formats

- ❑ Connect students to websites that contain content and strategies that support critical-thinking skills.

- ❑ Teach students to evaluate their research sources, particularly websites, and judge their credibility.

- ❑ Research critical-thinking concepts and find templates to use as rubrics for students.

- ❑ Embed global thinking into collaborative lessons.

- ❑ Locate and administer a thinking skills assessment or achievement test for student self-knowledge.

- ❑ Focus collaborative lessons on teaching the skills of argument analysis, problem-solving, decision-making, and cognitive process.

Action 1.3.b "Take Action" Tips

stays abreast of emerging technologies and formats

- ❑ Access resources, blog posts, and webinars supporting AASL's Best Websites for Teaching and Learning.

- ❑ Read library and technology journals for technology and social media tips.

- ❑ Subscribe to technology magazines.

- ❑ Set up alerts or RSS feeds for articles about teaching and technology.

- ❑ Add technology blogs to your PLN (Personal Learning Network).

- ❑ Join an ALA subgroup and add it to your PLN.

- ❑ Attend public library or other local tech training opportunities.

- ❑ Meet periodically with IT staff to discuss purchases, certificates of training, and emerging technologies.

Action 1.3.c "Take Action" Tips

integrates the use of state-of-the-art and emerging technologies as a means for effective and creative learning

- ❑ Collaborate with teachers and show them how to integrate new formats into their lessons.

- ❑ Allow students to check in/out their own materials at convenient stations in the library.

- ❑ Encourage the use of free, online collaboration tools including Web browsers (e.g., Mozilla Firefox), word processing tools (e.g., Google Docs), spreadsheet tools (e.g., Gelsheet), website authoring applications, personal learning networks, and e-mail.

- ❑ Take advantage of blended-learning opportunities by creating an online library course for your students using an open-source electronic learning-management system (e.g., Moodle, Sakai).

- ❑ Create learning nooks in the library space where students can practice using resources in multiple formats during free time, before, during, and after school.

❏ Create a student technology club that researches and discusses the latest technology and meets for lunch periodically.

❏ Create a technology collection for students to browse or borrow, and include magazines, brochures and equipment.

❏ Work to unblock educational websites and social media tools.

❏ Search for innovative methods to use current and emerging technologies to improve students' learning experiences.

❏ Help students access AASL's Best Websites for Teaching and Learning to find free emerging online tools that foster the qualities of innovation, creativity, active participation, and collaboration.

Action 1.3.d "Take Action" Tips

guides students and teachers to formats most appropriate for the learning task

❏ Create posters that show how to align social media formats to appropriate student products, and hang the posters in the library space to guide student work.

❏ Offer 15-minute afterschool technology "one-shots" for teachers to match technology formats to the right student products

❏ Push technology website links and articles to teachers.

Action 1.3.e "Take Action" Tips

embeds key concepts of legal, ethical and social responsibilities in accessing, using and creating information in various formats

❏ Include ethical polices on your library website, your social media page, and your learning-management system.

❏ Post material about evaluation criteria tools, citation formats, and acceptable-use policy (AUP) forms on your website, your social media page, and your learning management system (e.g., Moodle, Blackboard).

❏ Explain fair use with regard to illustrations and other nonprint materials.

❏ Share current stories about people caught violating research ethics and discuss accountability.

❏ Remind students about the school's academic integrity policy contained in the student handbook and point out the consequences of plagiarism.

❏ Ask principals and technology teachers to address students about plagiarism.

❏ Invite an academic librarian to share with your students college policies on the topics of plagiarism, citation styles, and intellectual freedom.

❏ Explain the concept of digital citizenry to your students.

❏ Create posters, displays, and lessons to remind staff and students that resources in all formats—including printed text, oral and electronic resources, slides, and visuals—need to be cited.

❏ Include information-literacy instruction throughout collaborative lessons.

❏ Encourage students to choose the subjects of plagiarism, copyright, fair use, academic integrity, authorship, and intellectual freedom as research topics, and create products that can be used as teaching tools.

1.3 TEACHING FOR LEARNING: Addressing Multiple Literacies

Action 1.3.f "Take Action" Tips

provides instruction specific to searching for information in various formats

- ❏ Create a set of webpages that contain subject guides and pathfinders to guide inquiry research (e.g., LibGuides, SubjectsPlus).

- ❏ Help teachers and students to create pathfinders and subject guides in conjunction with their inquiry-research projects.

- ❏ Purchase "how to" books and locate websites about use of emerging technologies for instructional purposes.

- ❏ Invite an academic librarian to show students how to navigate a college library website to find and use information in multiple formats.

- ❏ Use online tools to teach students how to refine their inquiry research with the incorporation of Boolean search strategies.

Action 1.3.g "Take Action" Tips

adapts to and models new skills, new technologies, and new understandings of the learning process

- ❏ Locate website content and lessons to teach critical-thinking skills to students.

- ❏ Use print and electronic graphic organizers including flowcharts, Venn diagrams, and Web 2.0 brainstorming tools (e.g., Bubbl.us, MindMeister) to help students organize their research facts and ideas.

- ❏ Use information literacy models such as the Big6 and D.I.A.L.O.G.U.E. to guide research.

- ❏ Scaffold collaborative lessons and build upon prior learning.

- ❏ Integrate learning styles (e.g., spatial) and multiple intelligences (e.g., Interpersonal) into library lessons.

- ❏ Keep abreast of learning theory research (e.g., right/ left brain theory).

- ❏ Teach students to use the summarizing tool in their word processing program to aid reading comprehension.

- ❏ Use your personal e-reader tablet and netbook at school during student lessons to model use of emerging technology.

Action 1.3.h "Take Action" Tips

encourages the use of multiple formats to present data and information in compelling and useful ways

- ❏ Make sure collaborative lessons and student products include visual, digital, textual, and technological formats.

- ❏ Encourage students to use Web 2.0 tools to build and manage their own virtual space, including a portal, a personal learning network, and a personal portfolio.

1.3   TEACHING FOR LEARNING: Addressing Multiple Literacies

Action 1.3.i "Take Action" Tips

My Actions

collaborates with classroom teachers to embed skills associated with multiple literacies into lessons and curricular units

❑ Make sure students can create and interpret visual communication.

❑ Create lessons that contain images for students to analyze and display/post student-created visual representations.

❑ Provide links to the public library's large-print collection.

❑ Prepare bookmarks and handouts listing your available assistive devices.

❑ Purchase resources in multiple languages, such as Spanish versions of English classics.

❑ Provide audio and video versions of print texts for comparison and contrast.

❑ Encourage teachers to include in their lessons online content creation tools such as video-production and microblogging sites, and offer to help teachers and students learn to use these tools.

❑ Share library reading lists in an online document-sharing system, and invite students and teachers to add to them.

❑ Review netiquette, Internet safety, and ethical use of online social-media tools (e.g. Facebook, Twitter, Skype).

❑ Keep 21st-century skills in mind when creating collaborative lessons for student mastery.

❑ Include visual, digital, textual, and technological literacies in lessons and assignments.

COLLECT EVIDENCE

Multiple examples of "Evidence of Accomplishment" are located in the Appendix at the end of this workbook. Review the list of potential evidence and select items that document the work you already do in your library. Brainstorm ways that you can add new evidence to your practice. Enter the action you will be implementing below. Use the "My Evidence of Accomplishment" space to record and organize evidence of your practice that you've already collected or plan to collect. Create a portfolio and share it with your principal during the librarian evaluation process.

ACTION _____

_____ _____

_____

My Evidence of Accomplishment

_____

_____

_____

_____

_____

_____

_____

_____

_____

_____

_____

_____

_____

_____

_____

MY ACTION PLAN

Use the "My Action Plan" worksheet to guide your planning process to accomplish the guideline action. After digesting the readings, noting appropriate action strategies, and entering your evidence information, consider and record your goals, target audience, tasks, timelines, and professional development plans. Enter the action you will be implementing below and use the key in the sidebar to help you complete your plan.

ACTION _____

_____

_____

MY GOAL		Task 1	Timeline
		Task 2	Timeline
		Task 3	Timeline
	Goal Type: _____ My Target Audience: _____		
My Professional Development Plan			Venue

MY GOAL		Task 1	Timeline
		Task 2	Timeline
		Task 3	Timeline
	Goal Type: _____ My Target Audience: _____		
My Professional Development Plan			Venue

MY GOAL		Task 1	Timeline
		Task 2	Timeline
		Task 3	Timeline
	Goal Type: _____ My Target Audience: _____		
My Professional Development Plan			Venue

MY ACTION PLAN KEY:

Goal Type

Short-term
Long-term
Part of Strategic Plan
Professional Development
Leader Role
Instructional Partner Role
Information Specialist Role
Teacher Role
Program Administrator Role

My Target Audience

SCHOOL COMMUNITY:
Students
Teachers
Administrators
Advisory Committee
Planning Committee
Friends of the Library
Volunteers (Student/Adult)

EXTERNAL STAKEHOLDERS:
Parents
Local Community
Business Community
Public Library
Academic Library
State Community
National Community
Global Community

My Professional Development Venue

District In-Service
Local/Regional Conference
State Conference
AASL National Conference
Community Learning
College Course
Evidence Collection
Action Research
Readings

Task Timeline

This Week
This Month
This Grading Period
This Semester
This Year
Next Year
2–3 Year Plan

TEACHING FOR LEARNING:
Effective Practices for Inquiry

models an inquiry-based approach to learning and the information search process

SUGGESTED READINGS

Examine these readings to learn best practices for achieving this guideline. As you read, look for new strategies to expand your professional practice and use the "My Notes" space to record your ideas.

Ainsworth, L., and J. Christinson. 1998. *Student-Generated Rubrics: An Assessment Method to Help All Students Succeed.* Orangeburg, NY: Dale Seymour.

Alman, S., C. Tomer, and M. L. Lincoln. 2012. *Designing Online Learning: A Primer for Librarians.* Santa Barbara, CA: Libraries Unlimited.

American Association of School Librarians. 2011. "Essential Links: Resources for School Library Program Development: Standards and Guidelines." <http://aasl.ala.org/essentiallinks/index.php?title=Standards_and_Guidelines> (accessed March 11, 2012).

———. 2012. "Essential Links: Resources for School Library Program Development: Common Core State Standards." <http://aasl.ala.org/essentiallinks/index.php?title=Common_Core_State_Standards> (accessed March 18, 2012).

"Bloom's Digital Taxonomy." 2012. *Educational Origami.* <http://edorigami.wikispaces.com/Bloom%27s+Digital+Taxonomy> (accessed March 11, 2012).

Common Core State Standards Initiative. 2011. "Mission Statement." <www.corestandards.org> (accessed March 18, 2012).

Curwin, R. 2012. "How to Motivate Learning: Alternatives to Rewards." <www.helpuseducate.org/articles/26810/how-to-motivate-learning-alternatives-to-rewards> (accessed March 18, 2012).

Deskins, L. M. 2012. "Inquiry Studies: Needed Skills." *School Library Monthly* 28 (5): 20–23.

Donham, J. 2010. "Enduring Understandings—Where Are They in the Library's Curriculum?" *Teacher Librarian* 38 (1): 15–19.

CONTINUED ON PAGE 133

My Notes

TAKE ACTION

Use these "Take Action" tips to help you brainstorm strategies you'll implement in your library program. Record your ideas and plans in the "My Actions" space provided.

Action 1.4.a "Take Action" Tips

supports educational and program standards as defined by the local, state, and national associations

❑ Use *A Planning Guide for Empowering Learners* to evaluate your library program against AASL's nationally established program guidelines.

❑ Use AASL's *Learning4Life Implementation Toolkit* and, by focusing on small segments, integrate the learning standards and program guidelines into your program.

❑ Join AASL, ALA, and other professional library organizations to learn about and advance advocacy initiatives.

❑ Include references to your school library program standards in educational conversations with staff.

❑ Serve on curriculum committees that produce courses of study and include library academic content standards.

❑ Share the AASL Common Core crosswalks with teachers and administrators, and talk to them about application of standards across all curriculum areas.

❑ Attend professional development sessions on Common Core State Standards and the school library program to help you better understand the school librarian's role in implementation.

Action 1.4.b "Take Action" Tips

integrates the use of state-of-the-art and emerging technologies as a means for effective and creative learning

❑ Collaborate with teachers to show them how to integrate new formats into their lessons.

❑ Allow students to check out their own library materials at self-checkout stations around your library space.

❑ Help students access AASL's Best Websites for Teaching and Learning to find free emerging online tools that foster the qualities of innovation, creativity, active participation, and collaboration.

❑ Encourage the use of free, online collaboration tools for word processing, creating slideshows, authoring websites, creating personal learning networks, sending e-mail, etc. (e.g., Google Apps for Education, Mozilla Firefox, Gelsheet).

❑ Take advantage of blended-learning opportunities by creating an online library course for your students using an open-source electronic learning-management system (e.g., Moodle, Sakai).

❑ Create learning nooks in the library space where students can practice using multiple formats during their free time, before, during, and after school.

❑ Create a technology club that researches and discusses emerging technologies and meets for lunch periodically.

❑ Create a technology collection for students to browse or borrow, and include magazines, brochures and equipment.

❑ Work to unblock educational versions of social media and other Web 2.0 tools.

1.4 TEACHING FOR LEARNING: Effective Practices for Inquiry

Action 1.4.c "Take Action" Tips

adapts to and models new technologies and new understandings of the learning process

❑ Locate website content and lessons to teach critical-thinking skills to students.

❑ Use print and electronic organizers to help students organize their thoughts and facts.

❑ Urge your school to select an information-literacy model to guide research projects.

❑ Scaffold lessons and build upon the prior learning of your students.

❑ Integrate learning styles and multiple intelligences into lessons.

❑ Stay abreast of learning theory research.

❑ Use your personal e-reader, tablet computer, and netbook at school during student lessons to model emerging technologies.

Action 1.4.d "Take Action" Tips

designs learning tasks that incorporate the information search process

❑ Visit the resources featured in AASL's Best Websites for Teaching and Learning, and incorporate the tools into your lessons.

❑ Share information-literacy tutorials and videos with your students and teachers (e.g., Kent State University's T2C).

❑ Create templates for students to use at each level of the information-literacy model.

❑ Provide pathfinders on information literacy and help students create them about their individual research topics.

❑ Use print and electronic graphic organizers to help students narrow their focus.

❑ Share a research calculator product with teachers so they can help their students organize their process and product (e.g. College Research Project Calculators, such as INFOhio Ask, Act, Achieve and the University of Maryland's TRAC).

❑ Collaborate with teachers and students to create a common vocabulary of search terms (e.g., pathfinders, subject guides, Boolean search strategy).

Action 1.4.e "Take Action" Tips

builds upon learners' prior knowledge as needed for the learning task

❑ Find out what students know, as well as what they don't, using pretesting, brainstorming, and other assessment strategies.

❑ Write a grant to purchase student response systems (SRS or "clickers") to use in the library.

❑ Ask teachers to share their knowledge of what their students know as a part of your collaborative lesson planning.

❑ Research ways to activate prior knowledge and employ other strategies such as K-W-L, so you can incorporate them into your lessons.

❑ Help students who think better visually: for both teaching and assessment, use visual tools for organizing knowledge (e.g., concept maps, diagrams, outlines, mind maps, webs).

Action 1.4.f "Take Action" Tips

provides aids that help learners collect information and data

❏ Use Web 2.0 tools that generate timelines and mind maps, or support brainstorming to help students collect and organize data (e.g., Bubbl.us, Timetoast, MindMeister).

❏ Use wiki and blog features to collect qualitative data.

❏ Teach students to locate, not only quantitative data, but encourage the collection of qualitative data as well (e.g. blog responses and anecdotal polls).

❏ Ask students on the newspaper staff to help poll the student body on issues.

❏ Ask guest speakers to share their thoughts about public-opinion polls.

Action 1.4.g "Take Action" Tips

provides opportunities for learners to revise their work through feedback from educators and peers

❏ Use Web 2.0 tools for peer- and self-editing (e.g., readwritethink.org's peer editing checklists, Microsoft Word's Reviewing Tools for Peer Editing).

❏ Show students how to use the think-pair-share strategy when they are peer-editing.

❏ Try the "fish bowl" technique: two students model peer-editing, based on their rubric criteria, for a third student.

❏ Include a peer-edit section for student use on your school blogs and wikis.

Action 1.4.h "Take Action" Tips

uses formative assessments to guide learners and assess their progress

❏ Familiarize yourself with professional literature on formative assessment.

❏ Collaborate with teachers to use multiple assessment strategies: cooperative learning activities, demos, exit cards, "I learned" statements, interviews, journal entries, K-W-L charts, learning logs, oral attitude surveys, oral presentations, peer evaluations, problem-solving activities, products, questioning, quizzes, response groups, and self-evaluations.

Action 1.4.i "Take Action" Tips

stimulates critical thinking through the use of learning activities that involve application, analysis, evaluation, and creativity

❏ Stimulate critical thinking in your collaborative lessons by including multiple activities such as brainteasers, optical illusions, mind maps, and online simulations.

❏ Develop writing activities that use guided questions to support critical thinking.

Action 1.4.j "Take Action" Tips

uses differentiated strategies with respect to gender, reading ability, personal interests, and prior knowledge to engage learners in reading and inquiry

❏ Make sure your students have a choice of instructional materials and resources at all levels and for a range of abilities.

❏ Personalize your instruction to fit each learner and incorporate student interests into lessons.

❏ Integrate real-world and authentic venues and settings when appropriate.

Action 1.4.k "Take Action" Tips

My Actions

uses diagnostics, including observation, checklists, and graphic organizers, to identify zones of intervention

❏ Study Response to Intervention (RTI) research and then join your school's RTI team.

❏ Participate in virtual networks with other librarians to learn to implement strategies such as small-group instruction and checklists.

Action 1.4.l "Take Action" Tips

applies appropriate interventions to help learners perform tasks that they cannot complete without assistance

❏ "Chunk" assignments within your collaborative lessons into doable pieces of learning.

❏ Allow other adults in the classroom or library to work with students having trouble getting started.

❏ Provide a formal work plan for students, breaking down lesson assignments, using a calendar or timeline, and providing for frequent feedback.

❏ Watch for student avoidance behaviors and supply motivation as needed.

❏ Monitor students and make adjustments in your teaching as you present lessons.

COLLECT EVIDENCE

Multiple examples of "Evidence of Accomplishment" are located in the Appendix at the end of this workbook. Review the list of potential evidence and select items that document the work you already do in your library. Brainstorm ways that you can add new evidence to your practice. Enter the action you will be implementing below. Use the "My Evidence of Accomplishment" space to record and organize evidence of your practice that you've already collected or plan to collect. Create a portfolio and share it with your principal during the librarian evaluation process.

ACTION _____

_____

My Evidence of Accomplishment

MY ACTION PLAN KEY:

Goal Type

Short-term
Long-term
Part of Strategic Plan
Professional Development
Leader Role
Instructional Partner Role
Information Specialist Role
Teacher Role
Program Administrator Role

My Target Audience

SCHOOL COMMUNITY:
Students
Teachers
Administrators
Advisory Committee
Planning Committee
Friends of the Library
Volunteers (Student/Adult)

EXTERNAL STAKEHOLDERS:
Parents
Local Community
Business Community
Public Library
Academic Library
State Community
National Community
Global Community

My Professional Development Venue

District In-Service
Local/Regional Conference
State Conference
AASL National Conference
Community Learning
College Course
Evidence Collection
Action Research
Readings

Task Timeline

This Week
This Month
This Grading Period
This Semester
This Year
Next Year
2–3 Year Plan

MY ACTION PLAN

Use the "My Action Plan" worksheet to guide your planning process to accomplish the guideline action. After digesting the readings, noting appropriate action strategies, and entering your evidence information, consider and record your goals, target audience, tasks, timelines, and professional development plans. Enter the action you will be implementing below and use the key in the sidebar to help you complete your plan.

ACTION _____

_____ _____

_____

MY GOAL		Task 1	Timeline
		Task 2	Timeline
	Goal Type: _____	Task 3	Timeline
	My Target Audience: _____		
My Professional Development Plan			Venue

MY GOAL		Task 1	Timeline
		Task 2	Timeline
	Goal Type: _____	Task 3	Timeline
	My Target Audience: _____		
My Professional Development Plan			Venue

MY GOAL		Task 1	Timeline
		Task 2	Timeline
	Goal Type: _____	Task 3	Timeline
	My Target Audience: _____		
My Professional Development Plan			Venue

TEACHING FOR LEARNING:
Assessment in Teaching for Learning

Guideline

My Notes

performs regular assessment of student learning to ensure the program is meeting its goals

SUGGESTED READINGS

Examine these readings to learn best practices for achieving this guideline. As you read, look for new strategies to expand your professional practice and use the "My Notes" space to record your ideas.

American Association of School Librarians. 2007. "Standards for the 21st-Century Learner." <http://ala.org/ala/mgrps/divs/aasl/guidelinesandstandards/learningstandards/AASL_LearningStandards.pdf> (accessed May 23, 2011).

Ash, K. 2012. "Rethinking Testing in the Age of the iPad." *Education Week: Digital Directions.* <www.edweek.org/dd/articles/2012/02/08/02mobile.h05.html> (accessed May 23, 2012).

"Assessment Rubrics." n.d. <http://edtech.kennesaw.edu/intech/rubrics.htm> (accessed May 23, 2012).

Callison, D. 1998. "Authentic Assessment." *School Library Media Activities Monthly* 14 (5): 42–43, 50.

———. 1998. "Metacognition." *School Library Media Activities Monthly* 14 (7): 43–44.

———. 2007. "Portfolio Revisited with Digital Considerations." *School Library Media Activities Monthly* 23 (6): 43–46.

Duvall, S., K. Jaaskelainen, and P. Pasque. 2011. "Grassroots Google Tools: ePortfolio in Assessment and Curriculum Integration." *School Library Monthly* 27 (7): 23–25.

Fontichiaro, K. 2011. "Nudging toward Inquiry: Summative Assessment." *School Library Monthly* 27 (7): 12–13.

Gallaudet University. n.d. "Portfolios for Student Growth." <www.gallaudet.edu/clerc_center/information_and_resources/info_to_go/transition_to_adulthood/portfolios_for_student_growth.html> (accessed May 23, 2012).

George Lucas Educational Foundation. 2012. "Classroom Guide: Top Ten Tips for Assessing Project-Based Learning." <www.edutopia.org/10-tips-assessment-project-based-learning-resource-guide> (accessed March 18, 2012).

Gordon, C. A. 1999. "Students as Authentic Researchers: A New Prescription for the High School Research Assignment." *School Library Media Research* 2: 1–21.

CONTINUED ON PAGE 135

TAKE ACTION

Use these "Take Action" tips to help you brainstorm strategies you'll implement in your library program. Record your ideas and plans in the "My Actions" space provided.

Action 1.5.a "Take Action" Tips

implements critical analysis and evaluation strategies

❏ Encourage students to tweet their responses in place of written exit slips.

❏ Create rubrics using Web 2.0 and multimedia apps while collaborating with students and teachers.

❏ Lead a school-wide initiative for digital portfolios for students.

Action 1.5.b "Take Action" Tips

uses summative assessments of process and product in collaboration with teachers

❏ Tell students and teachers about quick, nontraditional summative assessment methods in e-formats such as creating book trailers.

❏ Include the use of self-inquiry tools such as double-column journal entries to evaluate student process.

❏ Use tablet computers to assess students by employing immediate feedback features such as screencasting to drive instruction.

❏ Promote student-generated rubrics to motivate students' intrinsic "buy-in."

Action 1.5.c "Take Action" Tips

solicits student input for the assessment of inquiry-based instructional units upon their completion

❏ Share with students self-reflection tools, such as suggestion boxes, electronic surveys and polling, and student response systems (SRS or "clickers"), so learners can help you evaluate collaborative units at the end of the project.

❏ Teach students metacognition skills before launching a unit by modeling "thinking about thinking" strategies.

❏ Offer students tools such as muddiest point, one-minute paper, journals, and focus groups to evaluate completed units.

Action 1.5.d "Take Action" Tips

solicits student input for post-assessment of inquiry-based instructional units

❏ Share self-reflection tools such as suggestion boxes, electronic surveys and polling, and student response systems (SRS or "clickers") with students so they can help you evaluate collaborative units at the end of the project.

❏ Teach students metacognition skills before launching a unit by modeling "thinking about thinking" strategies.

❏ Offer students tools such as muddiest point, one-minute papers, journals, and focus groups to evaluate both products and process of collaborative units.

❏ Help students to generate their own rubrics, boosting motivation, interest, and the quality of their products.

Action 1.5.e "Take Action" Tips

uses formative assessments that give students feedback and the chance to revise their work

❑ Create a step-by-step rubric for students to revise their work and allow class time for students to complete the rubric.

❑ Keep original and revised print and electronic student work to track improvement over time.

❑ Determine the extent to which collaboration improves student learning in your school; document your findings.

❑ Allow test retakes within specific parameters to motivate students to keep learning.

❑ Encourage students to reflect on their work by providing class time to jot down "thinking about thinking" in their notebooks and double-column journals, and model reflection yourself.

❑ Convince students to accept that ongoing feedback and revision are essential to the learning process.

Action 1.5.f "Take Action" Tips

uses performance-based assessments, such as rubrics, checklists, portfolios, journals, observation, conferencing, and self-questioning

❑ Introduce a "conferencing log" to track student conversations with your students about their progress with library-related assignments.

❑ Use performance-based assessments to evaluate authentic products such as cartoons, recipes, and inventions.

Action 1.5.g "Take Action" Tips

creates rubrics for student work that integrate curricular, informational, and critical thinking standards

❑ Familiarize yourself with a variety of student-learning standards, including the learning standards adopted by your state (e.g., AASL's *Standards for the 21st-Century Learner*, Common Core State Standards, Partnership for 21st Century Skills framework).

❑ Use electronic rubric generators to create rubrics appropriate for student assessments (e.g., RubiStar, TeAchnology).

Action 1.5.h "Take Action" Tips

documents student progress through portfolios that demonstrate growth

❑ Lead a school-wide initiative for digital portfolios for students.

❑ Make sure your collaborative lessons include a method to document student growth over time as a result of your evidenced-based practice lessons.

My Actions

COLLECT EVIDENCE

Multiple examples of "Evidence of Accomplishment" are located in the Appendix at the end of this workbook. Review the list of potential evidence and select items that document the work you already do in your library. Brainstorm ways that you can add new evidence to your practice. Enter the action you will be implementing below. Use the "My Evidence of Accomplishment" space to record and organize evidence of your practice that you've already collected or plan to collect. Create a portfolio and share it with your principal during the librarian evaluation process.

ACTION _____

_____

My Evidence of Accomplishment

MY ACTION PLAN KEY:

Goal Type

Short-term
Long-term
Part of Strategic Plan
Professional Development
Leader Role
Instructional Partner Role
Information Specialist Role
Teacher Role
Program Administrator Role

My Target Audience

SCHOOL COMMUNITY:

Students
Teachers
Administrators
Advisory Committee
Planning Committee
Friends of the Library
Volunteers (Student/Adult)

EXTERNAL STAKEHOLDERS:

Parents
Local Community
Business Community
Public Library
Academic Library
State Community
National Community
Global Community

My Professional Development Venue

District In-Service
Local/Regional Conference
State Conference
AASL National Conference
Community Learning
College Course
Evidence Collection
Action Research
Readings

Task Timeline

This Week
This Month
This Grading Period
This Semester
This Year
Next Year
2–3 Year Plan

MY ACTION PLAN

Use the "My Action Plan" worksheet to guide your planning process to accomplish the guideline action. After digesting the readings, noting appropriate action strategies, and entering your evidence information, consider and record your goals, target audience, tasks, timelines, and professional development plans. Enter the action you will be implementing below and use the key in the sidebar to help you complete your plan.

ACTION _____

_____

_____

MY GOAL

	Task 1	Timeline
	Task 2	Timeline
	Task 3	Timeline

Goal Type: _____
My Target Audience: _____

My Professional Development Plan	Venue

MY GOAL

	Task 1	Timeline
	Task 2	Timeline
	Task 3	Timeline

Goal Type: _____
My Target Audience: _____

My Professional Development Plan	Venue

MY GOAL

	Task 1	Timeline
	Task 2	Timeline
	Task 3	Timeline

Goal Type: _____
My Target Audience: _____

My Professional Development Plan	Venue

BUILDING THE LEARNING ENVIRONMENT:
Planning and Evaluating

Guideline

helps to develop a long-term strategic plan that reflects the mission, goals, and objectives of the school

My Notes

SUGGESTED READINGS

Examine these readings to learn best practices for achieving this guideline. As you read, look for new strategies to expand your professional practice and use the "My Notes" space to record your ideas.

Adams, H. R. 2009. "Privacy Checklist: Evaluating the Library Media Program." *School Library Media Activities Monthly* 25 (7): 55.

American Association of School Librarians. 2009. *Empowering Learners: Guidelines for School Library Programs.* Chicago: ALA.

———. 2010. *A Planning Guide for Empowering Learners with School Library Program Assessment Rubric.* Chicago: AASL.

Anderson, Lisa. 2008. "Strategic Planning for Your District or School Library." *Indiana Libraries* 27 (2): 78–79.

Ballard, S. D., G. March, and J. K. Sand. 2009. "Creation of a Research Community in a K–12 School System Using Action Research and Evidence-Based Practice." *Evidence-Based Library and Information Practice* 4 (2): 8–36.

Brodie, C. S. 2002. "Setting Goals: the Road Not Yet Taken." *School Library Media Activities Monthly* 18 (6): 35, 47.

Church, A. 2003. *Leverage Your Library Program to Raise Test Scores: A Guide for Library Media Specialists, Principals, Teachers, and Parents.* Worthington, OH: Linworth.

Crowley, John D. 2011. *Developing a Vision: Strategic Planning for the School Librarian in the 21st Century,* 2nd ed. Santa Barbara: Libraries Unlimited.

Dickinson, G. K. 2005. "How One Child Learns: The Teacher Librarian as Evidence-Based Practitioner." *Teacher Librarian* 33 (1): 16–20.

Geitgey, G. A., and A. E. Tepe. 2007. "Can You Find the Evidence-Based Practice in Your School Library?" *Library Media Connection* 25 (6): 10–12.

Green, R. 2011. *Case Study Research: A Program Evaluation Guide for Librarians.* Santa Barbara, CA: Libraries Unlimited.

Johnson, D. 2001. "What Gets Measured Gets Done: The Importance of Evaluating Your Library Media Program." *Book Report* 20 (2): 14–15.

CONTINUED ON PAGE 136

2.1 BUILDING THE LEARNING ENVIRONMENT: Planning and Evaluating

TAKE ACTION

Use these "Take Action" tips to help you brainstorm strategies you'll implement in your library program. Record your ideas and plans in the "My Actions" space provided.

Action 2.1.a "Take Action" Tips

uses strategic planning for the continuous improvement of the program

❏ Lobby for a strategic library plan and make sure the school library is part of the district strategic plan.

❏ Ask your library advisory committee to help you create the strategic library plan to ensure buy-in of stakeholders.

❏ Use AASL's *A Planning Guide for Empowering Learners* to help you establish an entry point for setting program goals and action plans in a continuous improvement model.

Action 2.1.b "Take Action" Tips

develops, with input from the school community, mission statements and goals for the school library program that support the mission, goals, and objectives of the school

❏ Study a variety of strategic plan formats before choosing one for your library; consider creating an e-version of the plan.

❏ Make sure your mission and vision statements are tied to the school and district missions and vision statements.

Action 2.1.c "Take Action" Tips

writes objectives for each goal that include steps to be taken to attain the goal, a timeline, and a method of determining if the objective was attained

❏ Work through strategic library plan tutorials before trying to create a plan for your school library.

❏ Use AASL's *A Planning Guide for Empowering Learners* to assess your program and the goals you create for your school library program, and complete each set of goals and objectives by establishing and following action plans.

Action 2.1.d "Take Action" Tips

conducts ongoing evaluation that creates the data needed for strategically planning comprehensive and collaborative long-range goals for program improvement

❏ Reference the evaluation-cycle illustration in AASL's *A Planning Guide for Empowering Learners* to help you create a timeline to guide ongoing evaluation of the school library program with the support of your school library planning committee.

❏ Use AASL's learning standards and program guidelines resources as the standard for school library program development.

❏ Use the *School Library Program Assessment Rubric* in AASL's *A Planning Guide for Empowering Learners* to measure your program and help you set long-range goals.

Action 2.1.e "Take Action" Tips

uses evidence of practice, particularly in terms of learning outcomes, to support program goals and planning

❑ Begin collecting evidence-based practice documentation to show your impact on student learning.

❑ Create a study in your building to determine what your teachers and students think about how the school library supports their learning.

Action 2.1.f "Take Action" Tips

uses action research, a tool of evidence-based practice, to provide methods for collection of evidence and input from users through interviews, surveys, observations, journaling, focus groups, content analysis, and statistics

❑ Begin using participatory action research, with the help of your library advisory committee, to collect evidence that your library impacts learning.

❑ Partner with a classroom teacher to document the learning that results from your collaborative units with evidence such as Works Cited pages.

Action 2.1.g "Take Action" Tips

analyzes the data and sets priorities articulated as goals

❑ View the charts and graphs you created in AASL's *A Planning Guide for Empowering Learners* for snapshots of your data and the health of your program.

❑ Participate on school-wide committees that use data-driven decision-making for planning and setting goals.

❑ Use data-driven, decision-making to inform your program planning, as you use evidence such as demographics, test results, state standards, and library automation software statistics.

❑ Convert your data into goals and use the information to continuously improve your school library program.

Action 2.1.h "Take Action" Tips

generates evidence in practice that demonstrates the efficacy and relevance of the school library instructional program

❑ Use the reports section of your library automation software to generate evidence such as curriculum mapping and materials used in the library.

❑ Use Web 2.0 tools, such as electronic calendars and other individual assistance tracking tools, to collect evidence of your practice.

2.1 BUILDING THE LEARNING ENVIRONMENT: Planning and Evaluating

Action 2.1.i "Take Action" Tips

uses research findings to inform decision making and teaching practices

- ❑ Participate in national, regional, and state school library association workshops on methods of collecting evidence of practice.

- ❑ Ask what has changed for your learners as a result of your inputs, intervention activities, and process; focus on what your students have learned, not what you do.

- ❑ Choose library conference sessions to teach you how to find the evidence-based research you need to support your decision making.

- ❑ Review your teaching practices and decide which ones are reflective of current research about best practices.

Action 2.1.j "Take Action" Tips

plans for the future through data collection, program evaluation, and strategic planning

- ❑ Base your library program goals on the data you have collected about your impact on student learning.

- ❑ Use the results of library program evaluations, such as surveys, to plan future initiatives.

- ❑ Stick to your strategic planning goals that were based on evidence.

- ❑ Be ready to adjust when change occurs by using data collection and program evaluation tools.

My Actions

_____

_____

_____

_____

_____

_____

_____

_____

_____

_____

_____

_____

_____

_____

_____

_____

_____

_____

_____

_____

_____

_____

_____

COLLECT EVIDENCE

Multiple examples of "Evidence of Accomplishment" are located in the Appendix at the end of this workbook. Review the list of potential evidence and select items that document the work you already do in your library. Brainstorm ways that you can add new evidence to your practice. Enter the action you will be implementing below. Use the "My Evidence of Accomplishment" space to record and organize evidence of your practice that you've already collected or plan to collect. Create a portfolio and share it with your principal during the librarian evaluation process.

ACTION _____

_____   _____

_____

My Evidence of Accomplishment

MY ACTION PLAN KEY:

Goal Type

Short-term
Long-term
Part of Strategic Plan
Professional Development
Leader Role
Instructional Partner Role
Information Specialist Role
Teacher Role
Program Administrator Role

My Target Audience

SCHOOL COMMUNITY:
Students
Teachers
Administrators
Advisory Committee
Planning Committee
Friends of the Library
Volunteers (Student/Adult)

EXTERNAL STAKEHOLDERS:
Parents
Local Community
Business Community
Public Library
Academic Library
State Community
National Community
Global Community

My Professional Development Venue

District In-Service
Local/Regional Conference
State Conference
AASL National Conference
Community Learning
College Course
Evidence Collection
Action Research
Readings

Task Timeline

This Week
This Month
This Grading Period
This Semester
This Year
Next Year
2–3 Year Plan

MY ACTION PLAN

Use the "My Action Plan" worksheet to guide your planning process to accomplish the guideline action. After digesting the readings, noting appropriate action strategies, and entering your evidence information, consider and record your goals, target audience, tasks, timelines, and professional development plans. Enter the action you will be implementing below and use the key in the sidebar to help you complete your plan.

ACTION _____

_____ _____

_____

MY GOAL		Task 1	Timeline
		Task 2	Timeline
	Goal Type: _____	Task 3	Timeline
	My Target Audience: _____		
My Professional Development Plan			Venue

MY GOAL		Task 1	Timeline
		Task 2	Timeline
	Goal Type: _____	Task 3	Timeline
	My Target Audience: _____		
My Professional Development Plan			Venue

MY GOAL		Task 1	Timeline
		Task 2	Timeline
	Goal Type: _____	Task 3	Timeline
	My Target Audience: _____		
My Professional Development Plan			Venue

Guideline

part of a staff that includes a minimum of one full-time certified/licensed school librarian supported by qualified staff sufficient for the school's instructional programs, services, facilities, size, and number of teachers and students

SUGGESTED READINGS

Examine these readings to learn best practices for achieving this guideline. As you read, look for new strategies to expand your professional practice and use the "My Notes" space to record your ideas.

American Association of School Librarians. 2007. "L4L Sample Job Descriptions–School Librarian." <http://connect.ala.org/files/44286/sample_job_description_l4l_pdf_13839.pdf> (accessed June 7, 2012).

———. 2011. "Performance Evaluation Of School Librarians." <http://aasl.ala.org/essentiallinks/index.php?title=Performance_Evaluation_of_School_Librarians> (accessed March 7, 2012).

———. 2011. "Standards and Guidelines." <http://aasl.ala.org/essentiallinks/index.php?title=Standards_and_Guidelines> (accessed March 7, 2012).

Ballard, S. 2009. "Developing the Vision: An L4L Job Description for the 21st Century." *Knowledge Quest* 38 (2): 78–82.

Bertland, L. n.d. "Job Descriptions–School Librarians." <www.sldirectory.com/libsf/resf/evaluate.html#jobs> (accessed June 7, 2012).

Castro, J. 2010. "Are We Speaking the Same Language? Librarians, Principals, the School Library Program, and Taking the Lead." *Texas Library Journal* 86 (1): 20–21.

Johnson, D. 2010. "State Staffing Requirements." <http://dougj.pbworks.com/w/page/18142589/State%20staffing%20requirements> (accessed March 9, 2012).

Lehman, K. B., and L. E. Donovan. 2011. *Power Researchers: Transforming Student Library Aides into Action Learners*. Santa Barbara, CA: Libraries Unlimited.

Levitov, D. 2010. "Educating School Administrators." *School Library Monthly* 26 (6): 45–47.

My Notes

CONTINUED ON PAGE 137

TAKE ACTION

Use these "Take Action" tips to help you brainstorm strategies you'll implement in your library program. Record your ideas and plans in the "My Actions" space provided.

Action 2.2.a "Take Action" Tips

writes job descriptions that outline the roles, responsibilities, competencies, and qualifications of library staff, including paraprofessionals, student aides, and community volunteers

- ❏ Use information found in research articles to drive the creation of library job descriptions.

- ❏ Check Learning4Life resources on the AASL website for job description samples and templates to use as guides.

- ❏ Write a job description for all positions, even if some are not currently filled, and make filling these positions a part of your strategic library plan.

- ❏ Align your professional library job descriptions with National Board for Professional Teaching Standards, and AASL learning standards and program guidelines.

Action 2.2.b "Take Action" Tips

works in collaboration with each staff member to evaluate job descriptions on a regular basis

- ❏ Involve your staff in the creation of their job descriptions so they'll buy in and fully grasp their responsibilities, positively impacting student learning as a result.

- ❏ Make the evaluation process a collaborative effort and provide a process for staff to create goals for themselves that support the library program and the school district mission.

Action 2.2.c "Take Action" Tips

analyzes the instructional program to determine appropriate staffing patterns

- ❏ Base staffing patterns on library program goals and collect evidence to support your recommendations.

- ❏ Poll administrators, teachers, support staff, students and other stakeholders to complete your study and involve your library planning committee in the process.

- ❏ Delegate to your staff and volunteers responsibilities that may have traditionally been the school librarian's, giving you more time to impact student learning.

Action 2.2.d "Take Action" Tips

provides appropriate training and support for student aides and volunteers

- ❏ Use your student volunteers to both support library goals and contribute to their own personal learning.

- ❏ Consider using an online open-source learning management system (e.g., Moodle, Sakai) to develop a blended class for student volunteers; provide resources and lessons, and include their library duties as performance-based evaluation.

2.2 BUILDING THE LEARNING ENVIRONMENT: Staffing

Action 2.2.e "Take Action" Tips

works with administrators to ensure that the program is adequately staffed with professional and supporting staff

❏ Invite your principal to the library often so he or she realizes the work necessary to achieve the library program goals, which, in turn, support the primary building goal of student learning.

❏ Share your evidence of student learning in the library with your principal on a regular basis via reports, e-mails, and anecdotes.

❏ Share AASL's *Position Statement on Appropriate Staffing for School Libraries* with your principal when discussing staffing standards for effective school library programs.

Action 2.2.f "Take Action" Tips

creates an environment of mutual respect and collaboration in which all staff members work toward the common goal of student learning

❏ Adopt a philosophy of collaboration and make sure it underscores all your communication and teaching practices.

❏ Strive to create a learning commons atmosphere in your physical and virtual library space to facilitate interdisciplinary learning through inquiry, collaboration, and creativity.

My Actions

_____

_____

_____

_____

_____

_____

_____

_____

_____

_____

_____

_____

_____

_____

_____

_____

_____

_____

_____

_____

_____

_____

COLLECT EVIDENCE

Multiple examples of "Evidence of Accomplishment" are located in the Appendix at the end of this workbook. Review the list of potential evidence and select items that document the work you already do in your library. Brainstorm ways that you can add new evidence to your practice. Enter the action you will be implementing below. Use the "My Evidence of Accomplishment" space to record and organize evidence of your practice that you've already collected or plan to collect. Create a portfolio and share it with your principal during the librarian evaluation process.

ACTION

My Evidence of Accomplishment

MY ACTION PLAN

Use the "My Action Plan" worksheet to guide your planning process to accomplish the guideline action. After digesting the readings, noting appropriate action strategies, and entering your evidence information, consider and record your goals, target audience, tasks, timelines, and professional development plans. Enter the action you will be implementing below and use the key in the sidebar to help you complete your plan.

ACTION _____

_____ _____

_____

MY GOAL		Task 1	Timeline
		Task 2	Timeline
	Goal Type: _____ My Target Audience: _____	Task 3	Timeline
My Professional Development Plan			Venue

MY GOAL		Task 1	Timeline
		Task 2	Timeline
	Goal Type: _____ My Target Audience: _____	Task 3	Timeline
My Professional Development Plan			Venue

MY GOAL		Task 1	Timeline
		Task 2	Timeline
	Goal Type: _____ My Target Audience: _____	Task 3	Timeline
My Professional Development Plan			Venue

MY ACTION PLAN KEY:

Goal Type

Short-term
Long-term
Part of Strategic Plan
Professional Development
Leader Role
Instructional Partner Role
Information Specialist Role
Teacher Role
Program Administrator Role

My Target Audience

SCHOOL COMMUNITY:
Students
Teachers
Administrators
Advisory Committee
Planning Committee
Friends of the Library
Volunteers (Student/Adult)

EXTERNAL STAKEHOLDERS:
Parents
Local Community
Business Community
Public Library
Academic Library
State Community
National Community
Global Community

My Professional Development Venue

District In-Service
Local/Regional Conference
State Conference
AASL National Conference
Community Learning
College Course
Evidence Collection
Action Research
Readings

Task Timeline

This Week
This Month
This Grading Period
This Semester
This Year
Next Year
2–3 Year Plan

2.3 BUILDING THE LEARNING ENVIRONMENT: Learning Space

Guideline

provides flexible and equitable access to physical and virtual collections of resources that support the school curriculum and meet the diverse needs of all learners

SUGGESTED READINGS

Examine these readings to learn best practices for achieving this guideline. As you read, look for new strategies to expand your professional practice and use the "My Notes" space to record your ideas.

American Association of School Librarians. 2011. "Facilities." <http://aasl.ala.org/essentiallinks/index.php?title=Facilities> (accessed March 10, 2012).

———. 2011. "Flexible Scheduling." 2011. <http://aasl.ala.org/essentiallinks/index.php?title=Flexible_Scheduling> (accessed March 10, 2012).

———. 2012. "Intellectual Freedom." <http://aasl.ala.org/essentiallinks/index.php?title=Intellectual_Freedom> (accessed March 10, 2012).

———. 2012. "Technology." <http://aasl.ala.org/essentiallinks/index.php?title=Technology> (accessed June 8, 2012).

Baule, S. M. 2008. *Facilities Planning for School Library Media and Technology Centers*, 2nd ed. Worthington, OH: Linworth.

"Collaborator and Learning Commons Queen: Carol Koechlin Speaks." 2011. *Teacher Librarian* 38 (4): 62–63.

Erikson, R., and C. Markuson. 2007. *Designing a School Library Media Center for the Future*. Chicago: ALA.

Franklin, P., and C. G. Stephens. 2007. "Creating Webpages for the 21st Century Library Media Center." *School Library Media Activities Monthly* 24 (3): 41–42.

Harland, P. C. 2011. *The Learning Commons: Seven Simple Steps to Transform Your Library*. Santa Barbara, CA: Libraries Unlimited.

Harper, M. 2007. "How Physical Design Can Influence Copyright Compliance." *Knowledge Quest* 35 (3): 30–32.

Hawaii Department of Education, Network Support Services Branch. 2008. "School Technology Plan Templates." <http://nssb.k12.hi.us/tech_plan/index.html> (accessed March 10, 2011).

My Notes

CONTINUED ON PAGE 137

TAKE ACTION

Use these "Take Action" tips to help you brainstorm strategies you'll implement in your library program. Record your ideas and plans in the "My Actions" space provided.

Action 2.3.a "Take Action" Tips

ensures that library hours provide optimum access for learners and other members of the school community

❑ Keep the library accessible to students, parents, and the community 24–7 in a virtual environment.

❑ Use time before and after school, and during lunch periods to maximize in-library access for the school community.

❑ Collaborate with public librarians by sharing curriculum and projects so that they can support student learning too.

Action 2.3.b "Take Action" Tips

creates a friendly, comfortable, well-lit, aesthetically pleasing, and ergonomic space that is centrally located and well integrated with the rest of the school

❑ Study the library literature about learning commons and devise a step-by-step plan to use these principles to convert your space.

❑ Eliminate any unfriendly practices now in place and determine what "barriers to access" you can remove.

Action 2.3.c "Take Action" Tips

provides sufficient and appropriate shelving and storage of resources

❑ Put your bookshelves and tables on wheels to enable numerous and flexible configurations of your library space.

❑ Open up library storage and office spaces for use by the library learning community for meetings, small-group study, tutoring, advising, and curriculum meetings.

Action 2.3.d "Take Action" Tips

ensures that technology and telecommunications infrastructure is adequate to support teaching and learning

❑ Work with your state library to obtain funding and grants to increase your e-resources (e.g., Library Services and Technology Act).

❑ Set up periodic meetings with your information technology (IT) staff to make sure your program goals are met.

❑ Use free social media and open-source tools.

2.3 BUILDING THE LEARNING ENVIRONMENT: Learning Space

Action 2.3.e "Take Action" Tips

provides space and seating that enhance and encourage technology use, leisure reading and browsing, and use of materials in all formats

- ❏ Encourage students to use the study and reading nooks you created in your library by rearranging your physical space.

- ❏ Consider intershelving all formats of a title (e.g., paperbacks, hardbacks, DVDs, and audiobooks) side-by-side on the shelf so students can compare multiple formats.

- ❏ Rearrange your library space to make more room for new technologies.

- ❏ Place netbooks around the library, when not in use in the classroom, for student convenience.

Action 2.3.f "Take Action" Tips

promotes flexible scheduling of the school library facility to allow for efficient and timely integration of resources into the curriculum

- ❏ If you are currently on a fixed library schedule, begin an initiative to allow at least some time for open access and solicit the support of teachers who want to collaborate with you on Common Core State Standards lessons.

- ❏ Share AASL's *Position Statement on Flexible Scheduling* with your principal when discussing scheduling standards for effective school library programs.

- ❏ Start an extended hours program such as an afterschool or lunch-access program.

- ❏ Work with the public library to write a grant to support a "beyond the school day" program in your library for homework help or family literacy.

- ❏ Convert you back room or office space for a new purpose such as a video production room to accommodate your learners.

Action 2.3.g "Take Action" Tips

designs and maintains a library website that provides 24-7 access to digital information resources, instructional interventions, reference services, links to other libraries and academic sites, information for parents, and exhibits of exemplary student work

- ❏ Create a school library website on your school server or choose a free, open-source virtual space.

- ❏ Collaborate with your school's website design classroom teacher for student support of your library website.

- ❏ Make your library website interactive by including book review software that allows students and teachers to upload their personal reviews, blogs, and output from other Web 2.0 tools.

Action 2.3.h "Take Action" Tips	My Actions

creates an environment that is conducive to active and participatory learning, resource-based learning, and collaboration with teaching staff

❑ Create a learning environment where students can think critically, creatively, and ethically.

❑ Ask your library advisory committee to download a free, online design software program to create a visual layout before you begin changing your physical space.

❑ Design a proposal to include the custodial staff in the plan to rearrange library space.

❑ Host breakfast gatherings in the school library to share resources with teachers and students.

❑ Extend invitations to clubs and organizations to meet in your conference room or study spaces.

❑ Invite the school nurse, speech tutor, drug counselor, and other support staff to work in your space and share the "learning commons" with adults as well as students.

Action 2.3.i "Take Action" Tips

designs learning spaces that accommodate a range of teaching methods, learning tasks, and learning outcomes

❑ Provide signage that directs learners to the right resources and employ user-friendly terms such as "checkout desk," not "circulation desk."

❑ Prepare documentation guides, pathfinders, and getting-started sheets to help learners find information.

❑ Redesign your website to make access to resources less complicated and more user-friendly.

❑ Provide students with the supplies and tools they need and create "supply centers" at strategic points in the library space.

COLLECT EVIDENCE

Multiple examples of "Evidence of Accomplishment" are located in the Appendix at the end of this workbook. Review the list of potential evidence and select items that document the work you already do in your library. Brainstorm ways that you can add new evidence to your practice. Enter the action you will be implementing below. Use the "My Evidence of Accomplishment" space to record and organize evidence of your practice that you've already collected or plan to collect. Create a portfolio and share it with your principal during the librarian evaluation process.

ACTION _____

_____

My Evidence of Accomplishment

_____

_____

_____

_____

_____

_____

_____

_____

_____

_____

_____

_____

_____

_____

_____

MY ACTION PLAN

Use the "My Action Plan" worksheet to guide your planning process to accomplish the guideline action. After digesting the readings, noting appropriate action strategies, and entering your evidence information, consider and record your goals, target audience, tasks, timelines, and professional development plans. Enter the action you will be implementing below and use the key in the sidebar to help you complete your plan.

ACTION _____

_____

_____

MY GOAL		Task 1	Timeline
		Task 2	Timeline
	Goal Type: _____	Task 3	Timeline
	My Target Audience: _____		
My Professional Development Plan			Venue

MY GOAL		Task 1	Timeline
		Task 2	Timeline
	Goal Type: _____	Task 3	Timeline
	My Target Audience: _____		
My Professional Development Plan			Venue

MY GOAL		Task 1	Timeline
		Task 2	Timeline
	Goal Type: _____	Task 3	Timeline
	My Target Audience: _____		
My Professional Development Plan			Venue

MY ACTION PLAN KEY:

Goal Type

Short-term
Long-term
Part of Strategic Plan
Professional Development
Leader Role
Instructional Partner Role
Information Specialist Role
Teacher Role
Program Administrator Role

My Target Audience

SCHOOL COMMUNITY:

Students
Teachers
Administrators
Advisory Committee
Planning Committee
Friends of the Library
Volunteers (Student/Adult)

EXTERNAL STAKEHOLDERS:

Parents
Local Community
Business Community
Public Library
Academic Library
State Community
National Community
Global Community

My Professional Development Venue

District In-Service
Local/Regional Conference
State Conference
AASL National Conference
Community Learning
College Course
Evidence Collection
Action Research
Readings

Task Timeline

This Week
This Month
This Grading Period
This Semester
This Year
Next Year
2–3 Year Plan

2.4 BUILDING THE LEARNING ENVIRONMENT: Budget

Guideline

manages sufficient funding to support priorities and make steady progress to attain the program's mission, goals, and objectives

SUGGESTED READINGS

Examine these readings to learn best practices for achieving this guideline. As you read, look for new strategies to expand your professional practice and use the "My Notes" space to record your ideas.

American Association of School Librarians. 2012. "Budget." <http://aasl.ala.org/essentiallinks/index.php?title=Budget> (accessed June 8, 2012).

———. 2012. "Library Funding." <http://aasl.ala.org/essentiallinks/index.php?title=Library_Funding> (accessed June 8, 2012).

———. 2012. "Standards and Guidelines." <http://aasl.ala.org/essentiallinks/index.php?title=Standards_and_Guidelines> (accessed June 8, 2012).

Anderson, L. 2008. "Strategic Planning for Your District or School Library." *Indiana Libraries* 27 (2): 78–79.

Dickinson, G. 2003. *Empty Pockets and Full Plates: Effective Budget Administration for Library Media Specialists.* Worthington, OH: Linworth.

———. 2004. "Budgeting As Easy as 1-2-3: How to Ask for—and Get—the Money You Need." *Library Media Connection* 22 (6): 14–17.

Jensen, A. 2008. "Presenting the Evidence: Librarian's Annual Report to the Principal." *Knowledge Quest* 37 (2): 28–32.

Kaplan, A. G. 2010. "School Library Impact Studies and School Library Media Programs in the United States." *School Libraries Worldwide* 16 (2): 55–63.

Maxwell, D. 2005. "Money, Money, Money: Taking the Pain Out of Grant Writing." *Teacher Librarian* 32 (3): 16–21.

Miller, P. 2003. "Budget-Stretching Ideas." *School Library Media Activities Monthly* 19 (6): 38–46.

Poinier, S., and J. Alevy. 2010. "Our Instruction DOES Matter! Data Collected From Students' Works Cited Speaks Volumes." *Teacher Librarian* 37 (3): 38–39.

My Notes

CONTINUED ON PAGE 138

TAKE ACTION

Use these "Take Action" tips to help you brainstorm strategies you'll implement in your library program. Record your ideas and plans in the "My Actions" space provided.

Action 2.4.a "Take Action" Tips

creates a budget that ensures the library is adequately funded to support the program guidelines

❏ Rethink every section of your budget with the primary goal of supporting learning; if it's not used, don't replace or update it.

❏ Keep your program guidelines in mind as you prioritize your budget to support student learning.

Action 2.4.b "Take Action" Tips

meets regularly with the school principal and/or district chief financial officer to discuss the library budget

❏ Tie your budget requests to improving learning.

❏ Bring evidence of learning improvements to budget meetings, and involve student and parent advocates.

❏ Use evidence, such as poll results from all your stakeholder groups, to persuade your principal.

❏ Print the charts and graphs from your program assessment in AASL's *A Planning Guide for Empowering Learners* as visual snapshots to show your principal while making a case for budget needs.

Action 2.4.c "Take Action" Tips

collects current market data about information resource costs and shares the information with decision makers, such as site councils, administrators, and district financial officers

❏ Join consortiums to take advantage of vendors' group discounts on resources and supplies.

❏ Maintain collaborative relations with vendors to take advantage of best prices and complimentary services.

❏ Locate and use free resources to save library funds; take advantage of online citation generators and free e-books.

❏ Talk to a variety of vendors to get competitive pricing and take advantage of trial periods offered by e-database publishers.

Action 2.4.d "Take Action" Tips

seeks additional funding through fundraisers, grant writing, and parent donation programs

❏ Collaborate with your teachers and school district grant writers to generate library funds and learn about the grant-writing process.

❏ Lead your library advisory committee's efforts to obtain additional dollars through fundraisers.

❏ Convince your parent-teacher organization to support the library by distributing Reading is Fundamental (RIF) books or sharing book fair earnings.

❏ Initiate a book donation program to celebrate birthdays and other special events.

2.4 BUILDING THE LEARNING ENVIRONMENT: Budget

allocates funding through strategic planning to support priorities and make steady progress to attain outlined goals and objectives

❏ Tie your budget requests, especially increases or special funding, to the strategic plan.

❏ Include library funding needs in the action plans aligned with your program goals.

❏ Resubmit or move unfunded programs to the next year's budget to ensure "steady growth."

creates budget rationales and priorities using evidence from strategic planning.

❏ Tie your budget requests to your mission and goals, describe how budget items will improve learning, put the facts in reports and spreadsheets, and disseminate them.

❏ Analyze budget and proposal rejections and resubmit in a format that shows connections to student learning.

supports the budget with local and nationally published evidence that shows how the school library program impacts learning

❏ Research state studies of school libraries, find published evidence that supports how librarians impact student learning, and use it in your annual budget proposal.

❏ Share research studies with your library advisory committee so that members can begin helping you collect evidence to support your budget request.

❏ Participate in AASL's annual longitudinal study *School Libraries Count!*, and use your personalized results to make comparisons regionally and nationally in schools and districts with similar demographics.

My Actions

_____

_____

_____

_____

_____

_____

_____

_____

_____

_____

_____

_____

_____

_____

_____

_____

_____

_____

_____

_____

_____

_____

_____

_____

_____

_____

_____

_____

COLLECT EVIDENCE

Multiple examples of "Evidence of Accomplishment" are located in the Appendix at the end of this workbook. Review the list of potential evidence and select items that document the work you already do in your library. Brainstorm ways that you can add new evidence to your practice. Enter the action you will be implementing below. Use the "My Evidence of Accomplishment" space to record and organize evidence of your practice that you've already collected or plan to collect. Create a portfolio and share it with your principal during the librarian evaluation process.

ACTION   _____

_____   _____

           _____

My Evidence of Accomplishment

_____

_____

_____

_____

_____

_____

_____

_____

_____

_____

_____

_____

_____

_____

MY ACTION PLAN KEY:

Goal Type

Short-term
Long-term
Part of Strategic Plan
Professional Development
Leader Role
Instructional Partner Role
Information Specialist Role
Teacher Role
Program Administrator Role

My Target Audience

SCHOOL COMMUNITY:
Students
Teachers
Administrators
Advisory Committee
Planning Committee
Friends of the Library
Volunteers (Student/Adult)

EXTERNAL STAKEHOLDERS:
Parents
Local Community
Business Community
Public Library
Academic Library
State Community
National Community
Global Community

My Professional Development Venue

District In-Service
Local/Regional Conference
State Conference
AASL National Conference
Community Learning
College Course
Evidence Collection
Action Research
Readings

Task Timeline

This Week
This Month
This Grading Period
This Semester
This Year
Next Year
2–3 Year Plan

MY ACTION PLAN

Use the "My Action Plan" worksheet to guide your planning process to accomplish the guideline action. After digesting the readings, noting appropriate action strategies, and entering your evidence information, consider and record your goals, target audience, tasks, timelines, and professional development plans. Enter the action you will be implementing below and use the key in the sidebar to help you complete your plan.

ACTION _____

_____

MY GOAL		Task 1	Timeline
		Task 2	Timeline
		Task 3	Timeline
	Goal Type: _____ My Target Audience: _____		
My Professional Development Plan			Venue

MY GOAL		Task 1	Timeline
		Task 2	Timeline
		Task 3	Timeline
	Goal Type: _____ My Target Audience: _____		
My Professional Development Plan			Venue

MY GOAL		Task 1	Timeline
		Task 2	Timeline
		Task 3	Timeline
	Goal Type: _____ My Target Audience: _____		
My Professional Development Plan			Venue

73

BUILDING THE LEARNING ENVIRONMENT:
Policies

Guideline

develops and uses policies, procedures, and guidelines that support equitable access to ideas and information throughout the school community

My Notes

SUGGESTED READINGS

Examine these readings to learn best practices for achieving this guideline. As you read, look for new strategies to expand your professional practice and use the "My Notes" space to record your ideas.

Adams, H. R. 2007. "The Age of the Patron and Privacy." *School Library Media Activities Monthly* 23 (7): 35–36.

———. 2010. "The 'Overdue' Blues:' A Dilemma for School Librarians." *School Library Monthly* 26 (9): 48–49.

Agosto, D. E., and J. Abbas. 2011. *Teens, Librarians, and Social Networking: What Librarians Need to Know.* Santa Barbara, CA: Libraries Unlimited.

American Association of School Librarians. 2011. "Flexible Scheduling." <http://aasl.ala.org/essentiallinks/index.php?title=Flexible_Scheduling> (accessed March 12, 2012).

———. "Review Sources." 2011. <http://aasl.ala.org/essentiallinks/index.php?title=Review_Sources> (accessed March 13, 2012).

———. 2012. "Cataloging and Classification." <http://aasl.ala.org/essentiallinks/index.php?title=Cataloging_and_Classification> (accessed June 8, 2012).

———. 2012. "Censorship." <http://aasl.ala.org/essentiallinks/index.php?title=Censorship> (accessed June 8, 2012).

———. 2012. "Collection development—General." <http://aasl.ala.org/essentiallinks/index.php?title=Collection_Development_-_General> (accessed June 8, 2012).

———. 2012. "Ethical issues." <http://aasl.ala.org/essentiallinks/index.php?title=Ethical_Issues> (accessed June 8, 2012).

———. 2012. "Intellectual Freedom." 2012. <http://aasl.ala.org/essentiallinks/index.php?title=Intellectual_Freedom> (accessed June 8, 2012).

Bangerter, R., D. Keller, C. Harrick, and R. Huang, webinar presenters. 2011. "Plagiarism and the Web: Revisited." <http://pages.turnitin.com/Plagiarism_126_archive.html> (accessed March 13, 2012).

CONTINUED ON PAGE 139

TAKE ACTION

Use these "Take Action" tips to help you brainstorm strategies you'll implement in your library program. Record your ideas and plans in the "My Actions" space provided.

Action 2.5.a "Take Action" Tips

establishes school library program acquisition, processing, and cataloging procedures that conform with district policies

❑ Streamline your acquisition, processing, and cataloging procedures or delegate them to paraprofessionals, volunteers, and student aides to free you to impact student learning.

❑ Document your library procedures and share them with library support staff and volunteers.

❑ Buy preprocessed materials with digital records imported to your automated library software.

❑ Take advantage of vendor services such as collection mapping, age of collection reports, and reading level measurements.

❑ Teach your library team as many clerical skills as necessary to keep operations going smoothly behind the scenes.

❑ Set up self-checkout stations around the library.

Action 2.5.b "Take Action" Tips

establishes policies and procedures for the circulation of library materials

❑ Focus on open access for learners rather than on "preserving" the collection.

❑ Eliminate procedures that limit access, such as overdue fines, short circulation periods, inflexible schedules, closed periods, renewal bans, and restriction of materials due to age or ability levels.

❑ Allow students with "no way to pay" lost or damaged fees to work off their obligations by volunteering in the library where they can learn library skills authentically.

❑ Set up student checkout stations that free staff to help learners.

Action 2.5.c "Take Action" Tips

establishes policies for reserving and scheduling use of library spaces and resources

❑ Set up an equitable reservation and signout procedure for teachers and student groups who want to use library equipment.

❑ If the library is completely occupied, move to the classroom for book talks and citation instruction as part of a "learning on wheels" initiative.

❑ Encourage the use of mobile netbooks, e-readers, and tablet computers so "learning with technology everywhere" can take place anywhere in the building.

Action 2.5.d "Take Action" Tips

seeks input from appropriate members of the school community when developing policies

❏ Use the members of your library advisory committee to provide input on library policies and solicit opinions from their stakeholder groups, including faculty, administration, students, volunteers, parent-teacher organizations, parents, and the community.

❏ Gather input from stakeholders via electronic surveys and other data collection systems, and use the input to inform decision-making about library policies.

Action 2.5.e "Take Action" Tips

develops and implements board-approved collection development policies, including those for selection and purchasing

❏ Base your collection development policies on AASL and ALA position papers, learning standards and program guidelines, as well as your state's adopted standards.

❏ Tie your collection policy to your library, school, and district strategic plans—especially their missions, vision statements, and goals.

Action 2.5.f "Take Action" Tips

works with the technology department and school administrators to develop and implement acceptable-use policies

❏ Create acceptable-use policies (AUP) that reflect equal access and contemporary social-media philosophy about Web 2.0 e-resources, and publish a copy in the student handbook.

❏ Include access to social media and Web 2.0 tools that reflect the needs of 21st-century learners.

❏ Share the implications and consequences of your acceptable-use policy (AUP) with all students and keep on file their signed copies of the AUP.

Action 2.5.g "Take Action" Tips

works in conjunction with other school library professionals in the district to establish a reconsideration policy for challenged materials, which is adopted by the local board of education

❏ Use AASL and ALA resources as models for your reconsideration policy.

❏ Share your reconsideration policy with teachers and students to create a community of understanding about censorship.

2.5 **BUILDING THE LEARNING ENVIRONMENT: Policies**

works with faculty to develop policies that guide the ethical use of information

❑ Create an academic-integrity policy for students and teachers to internalize and sign, and put it in the student handbook.

❑ Address the concepts of censorship and plagiarism within the context of collaborative lessons and apply the concepts to student-generated products.

❑ Arrange with administrators for opportunities to educate teachers, students, and parents about ethical and acceptable use policies.

COLLECT EVIDENCE

Multiple examples of "Evidence of Accomplishment" are located in the Appendix at the end of this workbook. Review the list of potential evidence and select items that document the work you already do in your library. Brainstorm ways that you can add new evidence to your practice. Enter the action you will be implementing below. Use the "My Evidence of Accomplishment" space to record and organize evidence of your practice that you've already collected or plan to collect. Create a portfolio and share it with your principal during the librarian evaluation process.

ACTION _____

_____ _____

_____

My Evidence of Accomplishment

MY ACTION PLAN

Use the "My Action Plan" worksheet to guide your planning process to accomplish the guideline action. After digesting the readings, noting appropriate action strategies, and entering your evidence information, consider and record your goals, target audience, tasks, timelines, and professional development plans. Enter the action you will be implementing below and use the key in the sidebar to help you complete your plan.

ACTION _____

_____ _____

_____

MY GOAL

Goal Type: _____
My Target Audience: _____

	Task 1	Timeline
	Task 2	Timeline
	Task 3	Timeline

My Professional Development Plan | Venue

MY GOAL

Goal Type: _____
My Target Audience: _____

	Task 1	Timeline
	Task 2	Timeline
	Task 3	Timeline

My Professional Development Plan | Venue

MY GOAL

Goal Type: _____
My Target Audience: _____

	Task 1	Timeline
	Task 2	Timeline
	Task 3	Timeline

My Professional Development Plan | Venue

2.6 BUILDING THE LEARNING ENVIRONMENT: Collection and Information Access

Guideline

selects a well-developed collection of books, periodicals, and non-print material in a variety of formats that support curricular topics and are suited to inquiry learning and users' needs and interests

SUGGESTED READINGS

Examine these readings to learn best practices for achieving this guideline. As you read, look for new strategies to expand your professional practice and use the "My Notes" space to record your ideas.

Agosto, D. E. 2007. "Building a Multicultural School Library: Issues and Challenges." *Teacher Librarian* 34 (3): 27–31.

Ahart, M., K. Miller, A. Rominiecki, K. Smith, and S. Yates. 2011. "Linking Up L4L: Web Sites to Support the New AASL Standards in Your Library." *Teacher Librarian* 38 (3): 12–17.

Allen, M. 2010. "Weed 'Em and Reap: The Art of Weeding to Avoid Criticism." *Library Media Connection* 28 (6): 32–33.

American Association of School Librarians. 2011. "Collection Development—General." <http://aasl.ala.org/essentiallinks/index.php?title=Collection_Development_-_General> (accessed June 8, 2012).

———. 2012. "Banned Websites Awareness Day." <http://aasl.ala.org/essentiallinks/index.php?title=Banned_Websites_Awareness_Day> (accessed June 9, 2012).

———. 2012. "Filtering." <http://aasl.ala.org/essentiallinks/index.php?title=Filtering> (accessed June 9, 2012).

———. 2012. "Intellectual Freedom." 2012. <http://aasl.ala.org/essentiallinks/index.php?title=Intellectual_Freedom> (accessed June 8, 2012).

———. 2012. "Literacy." <http://aasl.ala.org/essentiallinks/index.php?title=Literacy> (accessed June 9, 2012).

American Library Association. 2012. "ALA Recommends..." <www.ala.org/offices/library/alarecommends/alarecommends> (accessed March 13, 2012).

———. 2012. "Banned Books Week: Celebrating the Freedom to Read." <www.ala.org/advocacy/banned/bannedbooksweek> (accessed March 13, 2012).

CONTINUED ON PAGE 140

My Notes

TAKE ACTION

Use these "Take Action" tips to help you brainstorm strategies you'll implement in your library program. Record your ideas and plans in the "My Actions" space provided.

Action 2.6.a "Take Action" Tips

advocates for and protects intellectual access to information and ideas

❏ Create an intellectual-freedom policy as part of your collection-development policy and post it in the library, classroom, and cyberspace.

❏ Work against initiatives and programs that block access to library print and e-resources.

❏ Implement library events such as Banned Websites Awareness Day, Banned Books Week, and Choose Privacy Week to support the concepts of intellectual freedom.

❏ Use AASL's intellectual freedom brochure as a tool when discussing such topics with stakeholders.

Action 2.6.b "Take Action" Tips

tracks inventory in the school library, taking advantage of up-to-date automation systems and keeping current with software releases and training

❏ Read literature available on collection development practices, such as AASL's *Collection Development for the School Library Media Program: A Beginner's Guide.*

❏ Take advantage of your library automation software module that includes a barcode inventory procedure and have student volunteers help with inventory.

❏ Use the inventory process to become acquainted with your collection, weed, and note areas to develop.

❏ Use the results of your inventory as supporting evidence for budget requests.

Action 2.6.c "Take Action" Tips

conducts regular weeding to ensure that the library collection is up to date

❏ Use proven methods such as CREW and MUSTIE to guide your weeding and teach weeding criteria to your library staff so they can help.

❏ Devise creative ways to share the materials you weed, such as showing the art department how they can recycle discarded books by turning them into art sculptures.

Action 2.6.d "Take Action" Tips

ensures the collection is centralized and decentralized as needed to support classroom activities and other learning initiatives in the school

❏ Link decentralized school buildings by electronically linking their resources on the library OPAC and transport print materials via intercampus mail.

❏ Encourage students to use self-checkout stations to request materials located in other spaces in the school district.

❏ If your school district is automated, loan materials from building to building so that your library resources get maximum usage.

Action 2.6.e "Take Action" Tips

promotes alternative reading options through reading lists, bibliographies, and webliographies that include periodicals, bestseller lists, graphic novels, books, and websites in multiple languages

❑ Share reading lists by posting them on your interactive 24–7 library website.

❑ Promote reading information generated by your school library OPAC and highlight the feature that reveals the most popular materials checked out by fellow students.

❑ Use a personalized dashboard publishing platform or a personal Web portal to create a "good reads" section on your library website (e.g., Netvibes, Pageflakes, Jog the Web).

❑ Subscribe to a reading advisory tool that helps students find read-a-likes (e.g., Goodreads, NoveList).

❑ Create webliographies and webpages with links to selected sites containing good reading lists.

Action 2.6.f "Take Action" Tips

links the digital library to local, regional, or state online networks, connecting with other public or academic libraries to take advantage of available virtual resources to support the school curriculum

❑ Examine other school websites to garner ideas for your library and search for social-media and Web 2.0 links to add.

❑ Include assistive features so students with disabilities can also learn from your website.

❑ Peruse AASL's Best Websites for Teaching and Learning for links to add to your website.

❑ Create links on your library webpage to public library and academic library catalogs in your area.

Action 2.6.g "Take Action" Tips

collaborates with the teaching staff to develop an up-to-date collection of print and digital resources in multiple genres that appeals to differences in age, gender, ethnicity, reading abilities, and information needs

❑ Seek new resources to enrich the curriculum and match students with the appropriate resources.

❑ Consider textual, visual, technological, and digital literacies when choosing print and e-resources.

❑ Add 21st-century formats to your collection, such as graphic novels, e-readers, and interactive book-review tools.

Action 2.6.h "Take Action" Tips

regularly seeks input from students through such tools as surveys and suggestion boxes to determine students' reading interests and motivations

❑ Poll students to learn their preferences before ordering new materials and motivate them by adding to the collection the latest popular series novels and nonfiction best sellers.

❑ Encourage students to share book reviews that support their reading recommendations because 21st-century students expect to participate in adding resources to their personal learning networks.

Action 2.6.i "Take Action" Tips

My Actions

maps the collection to ensure that it meets the needs of the school curriculum

❑ Use the collection-mapping tools provided in your library automation software.

❑ Enlist the help of your vendors to produce collection-mapping reports that describe your collection.

❑ Collaborate with stakeholders to meet every learner's needs.

Action 2.6.j "Take Action" Tips

reviews challenged materials using the reconsideration policy

❑ Contact your state school library association's challenge officer at the first sign of a formal challenge, so you are prepared to respond.

❑ Access resources at the ALA website created to support librarians dealing with challenged materials; resources include sample forms, hearing processes, strategies, and tips.

❑ If a challenge occurs, depend on the members of your preselected reconsideration committee to support the process.

❑ Make sure school personnel do not practice censorship by removing materials without going through the step-by-step reconsideration process established by the school board.

COLLECT EVIDENCE

Multiple examples of "Evidence of Accomplishment" are located in the Appendix at the end of this workbook. Review the list of potential evidence and select items that document the work you already do in your library. Brainstorm ways that you can add new evidence to your practice. Enter the action you will be implementing below. Use the "My Evidence of Accomplishment" space to record and organize evidence of your practice that you've already collected or plan to collect. Create a portfolio and share it with your principal during the librarian evaluation process.

ACTION _____

_____

_____

My Evidence of Accomplishment

_____
_____
_____
_____
_____
_____
_____
_____
_____
_____
_____
_____
_____
_____
_____
_____

Goal Type

Short-term
Long-term
Part of Strategic Plan
Professional Development
Leader Role
Instructional Partner Role
Information Specialist Role
Teacher Role
Program Administrator Role

My Target Audience

SCHOOL COMMUNITY:

Students
Teachers
Administrators
Advisory Committee
Planning Committee
Friends of the Library
Volunteers (Student/Adult)

EXTERNAL STAKEHOLDERS:

Parents
Local Community
Business Community
Public Library
Academic Library
State Community
National Community
Global Community

My Professional Development Venue

District In-Service
Local/Regional Conference
State Conference
AASL National Conference
Community Learning
College Course
Evidence Collection
Action Research
Readings

Task Timeline

This Week
This Month
This Grading Period
This Semester
This Year
Next Year
2–3 Year Plan

MY ACTION PLAN

Use the "My Action Plan" worksheet to guide your planning process to accomplish the guideline action. After digesting the readings, noting appropriate action strategies, and entering your evidence information, consider and record your goals, target audience, tasks, timelines, and professional development plans. Enter the action you will be implementing below and use the key in the sidebar to help you complete your plan.

ACTION _____

_____ _____

_____

MY GOAL		Task 1	Timeline
		Task 2	Timeline
		Task 3	Timeline
	Goal Type: _____ My Target Audience: _____		
My Professional Development Plan			Venue

MY GOAL		Task 1	Timeline
		Task 2	Timeline
		Task 3	Timeline
	Goal Type: _____ My Target Audience: _____		
My Professional Development Plan			Venue

MY GOAL		Task 1	Timeline
		Task 2	Timeline
		Task 3	Timeline
	Goal Type: _____ My Target Audience: _____		
My Professional Development Plan			Venue

2.7 BUILDING THE LEARNING ENVIRONMENT: Outreach

Guideline

implements an advocacy plan that builds support from decision makers who affect the quality of the school library program

SUGGESTED READINGS

Examine these readings to learn best practices for achieving this guideline. As you read, look for new strategies to expand your professional practice and use the "My Notes" space to record your ideas.

American Association of School Librarians. 2011. "Literacy." <http://aasl.ala.org/essentiallinks/index.php?title=Literacy> (accessed March 13, 2012).

———. 2011. "Volunteers." <http://aasl.ala.org/essentiallinks/index.php?title=Volunteers> (accessed March 13, 2012).

———. 2012. "AASL Advocacy Toolkit: The School Library: What Parents Should Know." <www.ala.org/aasl/aaslissues/toolkits/whatparentsshould> (accessed March 13, 2012).

———. 2012. "Advocacy—Policy Makers." <http://aasl.ala.org/essentiallinks/index.php?title=Advocacy_-_Policy_Makers> (accessed March 14, 2012).

———. 2012. "Toolkits." <www.ala.org/aasl/aaslissues/toolkits/toolkits> (accessed March 14, 2012).

American Library Association. 2012. "Form a Friends Group." <www.ala.org/advocacy/advleg/advocacyuniversity/toolkit/outreach/friendsgroup> (March 13, 2012).

Andrews, S. D. 2011. "Using National Data to Make Decisions as a Solo Librarian." *Knowledge Quest* 40 (2): 54–58.

Association of Library Trustees, Advocates, Friends and Foundations. "Friends & Foundations Fact Sheets." 2012. <www.ala.org/altaff/friends/factsheets> (accessed March 13, 2012).

Bush, G. 2007. "Telling Our School Library Story." *Knowledge Quest* 36 (1): 40–43.

Chen, D. R. 2007. "The Importance of the Library Media Specialist as a Political Voice." *School Library Media Activities Monthly* 23 (10): 46–48.

CONTINUED ON PAGE 141

My Notes

TAKE ACTION

Use these "Take Action" tips to help you brainstorm strategies you'll implement in your library program. Record your ideas and plans in the "My Actions" space provided.

Action 2.7.a "Take Action" Tips

forms a "Friends of the School Library" program

❑ Ask your building's parent-teacher organization members to be in your "Friends of the Library" group, based on their interest in reading initiatives and event-planning skills.

❑ Select your library planning committee members for qualities that support library program planning and setting library program goals.

Action 2.7.b "Take Action" Tips

encourages parents and community members to support learners by volunteering in the library

❑ Invite people from all your stakeholder groups—including parents, administration, teachers, students, and the community—to volunteer in the library.

❑ Give each volunteer an orientation program and handbook so that all members of the library team know their duties and understand the school library program standards.

❑ Create a written volunteer "job" description and make it a part of your school library volunteer policy.

Action 2.7.c "Take Action" Tips

participates in PTA/PTO or other school-based parent groups

❑ Use membership in your parent-teacher organization to both advocate for the school library and determine the needs of parents that you meet.

❑ Share your school library program goals with parents and encourage PTO members to participate in the library as volunteers or library advisory committee members, depending on their qualifications and interests.

❑ Ask to be placed on the parent-teacher organization agenda and make presentations about events and celebrations, such as School Library Month, and about the Reading is Fundamental (RIF) initiative.

❑ Use AASL's *Parent Advocate Toolkit* to help you gain parent support for your program.

Action 2.7.d "Take Action" Tips

encourages visits to and use of the library by parents, administrators, elected officials, and other stakeholders

❑ As a part of your school library program advocacy, invite a local legislator to your library to read to students for School Library Month, Read Across America, and other library events. (Invite the local newpaper's photographer, too.)

❑ Encourage community members, such as alumni or historical societies, to use resources in your library's historical section.

❑ Share with parents information about resources their children might need, such as audio versions of novels their children are struggling to read in print or "sick kid" kits with extended checkout.

❑ Consult AASL's "30 Days of Activities" calendar for ideas to attract stakeholders to the library during School Library Month, and for other events and initiatives.

❑ Employ the advocacy brochures from AASL's *School Libraries Improve Student Learning* series as tools to help guide discussion with stakeholders in your community, including teachers, administrators, parents, and policymakers.

Action 2.7.e "Take Action" Tips

attends department, curriculum, faculty, and other school- and district-based meetings

❑ Develop your instructional leadership by attending department, curriculum, standards, strategic planning, intervention, and technology meetings.

❑ Keep up to date with cutting-edge instructional strategies, including teaching, assessment and emerging technologies, so you can provide input at committee meetings.

Action 2.7.f "Take Action" Tips

communicates to stakeholders through the library website, parent newsletters, e-mail, and other formats

❑ Use your school e-mail or online grade book to keep parents aware of library issues and activities.

❑ Use a free online learning-management system (e.g., Moodle, Sakai) to push library information to students and parents.

❑ Use your library website to roll out new information and make the site interactive by including social-media tools and Web 2.0 links.

❑ Find templates and samples in the AASL/ALA Campaign for America's Libraries *Toolkit for School Library Programs* to help you generate ideas, and create messages and strategies for promoting the value of the school library program and school librarians in the twenty-first century.

Action 2.7.g "Take Action" Tips

offers to provide informational programs for community special-interest and service groups

❑ Provide programming that addresses the needs of groups in your community, such as hosting a FAFSA workshop about college financial aid.

❑ Work with your IT department to set up a cyber-safety program for parents to inform them about netiquette, AUPs, and stranger-danger on the Internet.

❑ Offer homework help programs, such as technology instruction for parents, and family literacy nights in the library.

2.7 **BUILDING THE LEARNING ENVIRONMENT: Outreach**

builds relationships with local, state, and national decision makers

❏ Take advantage of the chance to meet and advocate with educational leaders and legislators who attend state and national library conferences.

❏ Sign circulated petitions on library-advocacy issues, and call or e-mail your local legislators to support bills that impact school libraries.

❏ Participate in the annual National Library Legislative Day for schools in your state or in Washington, DC.

uses local, state, national, and international school library data to engage support

❏ Garner support for your school library by making stakeholders aware of the data from the numerous state studies that prove that school librarians impact student learning.

❏ Combine data from state and national research with your local evidence to build the case for school libraries.

❏ Participate in AASL's annual longitudinal study *School Libraries Count!* and use your personalized results to make comparisons regionally and nationally in schools and districts with similar demographics.

forms partnerships with the local and global community to promote student learning

❏ Join the national college and career readiness movement to make sure your students are ready to transition.

❏ Use information-literacy assessment tools designed to evaluate students' information literacy skills at all grade levels.

analyzes stakeholder goals and issues for potential alignment with library activities and resources, and builds promotional efforts around them

❏ Advocate for student learning, not school libraries and school librarians, and design your library program around the needs of stakeholders, not you.

❏ Distribute the advocacy brochures from AASL's *School Library Programs Improve Student Learning* series, which address each stakeholder audience with facts, statistics, goals, and key questions that are specific to the needs of that audience.

❏ Convert transitional library spaces created to serve library staff to service spaces that meet your program goals and the needs of your learning community (e.g. convert your storeroom to a video production studio so your students can create films).

2.7 BUILDING THE LEARNING ENVIRONMENT: Outreach

Action 2.7.1 "Take Action" Tips

writes articles and regular reports giving concrete evidence of what the library does to prepare learners to be successful in the twenty-first century

❏ Write articles for the student newspaper, the school district newsletter, and the local newspaper.

❏ Feature the accomplishments and learning of your stakeholders and describe how the library supported them.

❏ Access the "Create Your Own Story" webinars and handouts from the 2011 School Library Month archive on AASL's website to learn how to create strategic stories to gain support for your school library.

My Actions

_____

_____

_____

_____

_____

_____

_____

_____

_____

_____

_____

_____

_____

_____

_____

_____

_____

_____

_____

_____

_____

_____

_____

COLLECT EVIDENCE

Multiple examples of "Evidence of Accomplishment" are located in the Appendix at the end of this workbook. Review the list of potential evidence and select items that document the work you already do in your library. Brainstorm ways that you can add new evidence to your practice. Enter the action you will be implementing below. Use the "My Evidence of Accomplishment" space to record and organize evidence of your practice that you've already collected or plan to collect. Create a portfolio and share it with your principal during the librarian evaluation process.

ACTION _____

_____ _____

_____

My Evidence of Accomplishment

_____

_____

_____

_____

_____

_____

_____

_____

_____

_____

_____

_____

_____

_____

MY ACTION PLAN

Use the "My Action Plan" worksheet to guide your planning process to accomplish the guideline action. After digesting the readings, noting appropriate action strategies, and entering your evidence information, consider and record your goals, target audience, tasks, timelines, and professional development plans. Enter the action you will be implementing below and use the key in the sidebar to help you complete your plan.

ACTION _____

_____ _____

_____

MY ACTION PLAN KEY:

Goal Type

Short-term
Long-term
Part of Strategic Plan
Professional Development
Leader Role
Instructional Partner Role
Information Specialist Role
Teacher Role
Program Administrator Role

My Target Audience

SCHOOL COMMUNITY:
Students
Teachers
Administrators
Advisory Committee
Planning Committee
Friends of the Library
Volunteers (Student/Adult)

EXTERNAL STAKEHOLDERS:
Parents
Local Community
Business Community
Public Library
Academic Library
State Community
National Community
Global Community

My Professional Development Venue

District In-Service
Local/Regional Conference
State Conference
AASL National Conference
Community Learning
College Course
Evidence Collection
Action Research
Readings

Task Timeline

This Week
This Month
This Grading Period
This Semester
This Year
Next Year
2–3 Year Plan

MY GOAL

	Task 1	Timeline
	Task 2	Timeline
	Task 3	Timeline

Goal Type: _____
My Target Audience: _____

| My Professional Development Plan | Venue |

MY GOAL

	Task 1	Timeline
	Task 2	Timeline
	Task 3	Timeline

Goal Type: _____
My Target Audience: _____

| My Professional Development Plan | Venue |

MY GOAL

	Task 1	Timeline
	Task 2	Timeline
	Task 3	Timeline

Goal Type: _____
My Target Audience: _____

| My Professional Development Plan | Venue |

BUILDING THE LEARNING ENVIRONMENT: Professional Development

Guideline

engages in and provides support for school librarian and teacher professional development to sustain and increase knowledge and skills

SUGGESTED READINGS

Examine these readings to learn best practices for achieving this guideline. As you read, look for new strategies to expand your professional practice and use the "My Notes" space to record your ideas.

American Association of School Librarians. 2011. "Professional Periodicals." <http://aasl.ala.org/essentiallinks/index.php?title=Professional_Periodicals> (accessed March 14, 2012).

———. 2011. "Social Networking Guide. <http://aasl.ala.org/essentiallinks/index.php?title=Social_Networking_Guide> (accessed March 14, 2012).

Anderson, M. A. 2003. "Creating Tech-Savvy Teachers." *School Library Journal* 49 (2): 6–7.

Appleton, K., D. DeGroot, K. Lampe, and C. Carruthers. 2009. "Using Moodle: How Rural School Librarians Stay Connected." *School Library Monthly* 26 (2): 14–16.

Bates, J., J. McClure, and A. Spinks. 2010. "Making the Case for Evidence-Based Practice." *Library Media Connection* 29 (1): 24–27.

Bishop, K., and S. Janczak. 2005. "Conducting Effective Staff Development Workshops." *Library Media Connection* 23 (7): 50–51.

———. 2005. *Staff Development Guide to Workshops for Technology and Information Literacy: Ready-To-Present!* Worthington, OH: Linworth.

Bush, G., and J. L. Jones. 2011. "Revisiting Professional Dispositions: Research Redux." *School Library Monthly* 28 (2): 14–16.

Cox, E. 2011. "Workshop to Webinar: Revamping Professional Development." *School Library Monthly* 27 (5): 34–35.

Farmer, L. S. J. 2009. *Your School Library: Check It Out!* Westport, CT: Libraries Unlimited.

Fontichiaro, K. 2008. Planning an Online Professional Development Module. *School Library Media Activities Monthly* 25 (2): 30–31.

CONTINUED ON PAGE 142

My Notes

TAKE ACTION

Use these "Take Action" tips to help you brainstorm strategies you'll implement in your library program. Record your ideas and plans in the "My Actions" space provided.

Action 2.8.a "Take Action" Tips

reads research relevant to school libraries, student learning, and new developments in the educational field

❑ Access Library Literature & Information Science database articles with your local academic librarian and request a temporary guest password.

❑ Subscribe to top professional library journals, such as *Knowledge Quest, School Library Journal, School Library Monthly, Library Media Connection*, and *Teacher Librarian*, and put reading the articles on your weekly to-do list.

Action 2.8.b "Take Action" Tips

ensures access to professional development opportunities for professional and paraprofessional staff

❑ Supplement the traditional school in-service format with webinars and tutorials to professionally develop your staff, and link the resources to your library website, library companion site, and blended learning course.

❑ Use free online learning-management systems (e.g., Moodle, Sakai) to house information and policies you want stakeholders to access 24–7 at home or school.

Action 2.8.c "Take Action" Tips

takes advantage of professional development opportunities and shares new learning with the school administration and faculty

❑ Get on the agendas of teachers' meetings, department meetings, curriculum meetings, and board of education meetings to share new learning from your conference sessions and other professional development venues.

❑ Volunteer to help your IT staff when they schedule "Wired Wednesdays" or other technology training sessions. Promote these events on your library website and social-media page, and in your learning management system.

Action 2.8.d "Take Action" Tips

participates in and provides professional development to sustain and to develop knowledge and skills

❑ Build a virtual personal learning network (PLN) as a structure to organize your professional development and include blogs by library professionals, other professional learning networks, webinars, tutorials, and social media.

❑ Stretch your professional skills by teaching Post Secondary Education Option (PSEO) classes, adult education sessions, community college courses, and four-year college courses.

2.8 BUILDING THE LEARNING ENVIRONMENT: Professional Development

Action 2.8.e "Take Action" Tips

seeks opportunities to teach new skills to the faculty and staff, whether in a classroom setting or one-on-one instruction

❏ Use any opportunity to share your expertise with colleagues, such as during a collaborative lesson-planning session, over lunch in the teachers' lounge, or during spontaneous conversations.

❏ Offer quick one-to-one technology or inquiry-learning sessions after school or during planning periods; create a sign-up sheet with available time slots and post it on your website.

Action 2.8.f "Take Action" Tips

participates in local, regional, state, and national educational conferences as a learner and as a teacher

❏ Expand your personal learning network by attending as many professional development opportunities with colleagues as your administration and schedule permit, to form a career-support network.

❏ Use bookmarking (e.g., LiveBinders, Diigo, Delicious, Weave) and digital portfolio tools (e.g., Evernote, WordPress) to organize new information and resources, and push the new knowledge to your personal learning network.

My Actions

_____
_____
_____
_____
_____
_____
_____
_____
_____
_____
_____
_____
_____
_____
_____
_____
_____
_____
_____
_____
_____
_____
_____
_____
_____
_____

COLLECT EVIDENCE

Multiple examples of "Evidence of Accomplishment" are located in the Appendix at the end of this workbook. Review the list of potential evidence and select items that document the work you already do in your library. Brainstorm ways that you can add new evidence to your practice. Enter the action you will be implementing below. Use the "My Evidence of Accomplishment" space to record and organize evidence of your practice that you've already collected or plan to collect. Create a portfolio and share it with your principal during the librarian evaluation process.

ACTION

My Evidence of Accomplishment

MY ACTION PLAN KEY:

Goal Type

Short-term
Long-term
Part of Strategic Plan
Professional Development
Leader Role
Instructional Partner Role
Information Specialist Role
Teacher Role
Program Administrator Role

My Target Audience

SCHOOL COMMUNITY:
Students
Teachers
Administrators
Advisory Committee
Planning Committee
Friends of the Library
Volunteers (Student/Adult)

EXTERNAL STAKEHOLDERS:
Parents
Local Community
Business Community
Public Library
Academic Library
State Community
National Community
Global Community

My Professional Development Venue

District In-Service
Local/Regional Conference
State Conference
AASL National Conference
Community Learning
College Course
Evidence Collection
Action Research
Readings

Task Timeline

This Week
This Month
This Grading Period
This Semester
This Year
Next Year
2–3 Year Plan

MY ACTION PLAN

Use the "My Action Plan" worksheet to guide your planning process to accomplish the guideline action. After digesting the readings, noting appropriate action strategies, and entering your evidence information, consider and record your goals, target audience, tasks, timelines, and professional development plans. Enter the action you will be implementing below and use the key in the sidebar to help you complete your plan.

ACTION _____

___ _____

_____

MY GOAL

Task 1	Timeline
Task 2	Timeline
Task 3	Timeline

Goal Type: _____
My Target Audience: _____

My Professional Development Plan | Venue

MY GOAL

Task 1	Timeline
Task 2	Timeline
Task 3	Timeline

Goal Type: _____
My Target Audience: _____

My Professional Development Plan | Venue

MY GOAL

Task 1	Timeline
Task 2	Timeline
Task 3	Timeline

Goal Type: _____
My Target Audience: _____

My Professional Development Plan | Venue

 **3.1** **EMPOWERING LEARNING THROUGH LEADERSHIP: Leadership**

Guideline

My Notes

models professionalism, leadership, and best practice for the school community

SUGGESTED READINGS

Examine these readings to learn best practices for achieving this guideline. As you read, look for new strategies to expand your professional practice and use the "My Notes" space to record your ideas.

American Association of School Librarians. 2011. "School Reform." <http://aasl.ala. org/essentiallinks/index. php?title=School_Reform> (accessed March 16, 2012).

———. 2012. "Crosswalk of the Common Core Standards and the Standards for the 21st-Century Learner." <www.ala.org/aasl/ guidelinesandstandards/ commoncorecrosswalk> (accessed March 16, 2012).

———. 2012. "Join AASL." <www. ala.org/aasl/aboutaasl/ aaslmembership/ aaslmembership> (accessed March 16, 2012).

Baule, S. M., and J. E. Lewis. 2012. *Social Networking for Schools.* Santa Barbara, CA: Linworth.

Coatney, S., ed. 2010. *The Many Faces of School Library Leadership.* Santa Barbara, CA: Libraries Unlimited.

DiScala, J., and M. Subramaniam. 2011. "Evidence-Based Practice: A Practice towards Leadership Credibility among School Librarians." *School Libraries Worldwide* 17 (2): 59–70.

Downey, A., L. Ramin, and G. Byerly. 2008. "Simple Ways to Add Active Learning to Your Library Instruction." *Texas Library Journal* 84 (2): 52–54.

Fontichiaro, K. 2011. "Common Core Standards." *School Library Monthly* 28 (1): 49–50.

Frost, C. 2005. "Leadership: Library Leaders: Your Role in the Professional Learning Community." *Knowledge Quest* 33 (5): 41–42.

Hamilton, B. J. 2011. "Creating Conversations for Learning: School Libraries as Sites of Participatory Culture." *School Library Monthly* 27 (8): 41–43.

Harada, V. H., and S. Hughes-Hassell. 2007. "Facing the Reform Challenge: Teacher-Librarians as Change Agents." *Teacher Librarian* 35 (2): 8–13.

CONTINUED ON PAGE 143

TAKE ACTION

Use these "Take Action" tips to help you brainstorm strategies you'll implement in your library program. Record your ideas and plans in the "My Actions" space provided.

Action 3.1.a "Take Action" Tips

shares knowledge about libraries and learning by publishing articles in the school newsletter or other community news sources

❑ Participate in professional blogs, wikis, and social media sites such as the AASL Blog, as a first step towards publishing.

❑ Turn your library website into a publishing opportunity for both you and your stakeholders by adding a blog for their comments and your responses.

Action 3.1.b "Take Action" Tips

shares expertise by presenting information at faculty meetings, parent meetings, and school board meetings

❑ Begin your road to successful instructional and curriculum leadership by presenting at faculty, PTO, curriculum, strategic planning, and board of education meetings.

❑ Increase the impact of your presentations by using Web 2.0 tools to create brief slideshows that include video and audio clips of students at work in your library space.

Action 3.1.c "Take Action" Tips

fosters an atmosphere of respect and rapport between the school librarian and all members of the learning community to encourage student learning and to promote teacher enthusiasm and participation

❑ Support the philosophy that the library space, both virtual and physical, is a common area for self-paced learning, collaboration and content creation, as well as for accessing and sharing resources.

❑ Listen to teachers and other stakeholders, and make it your primary goal to support all learners—and remember that *everyone* is a learner.

Action 3.1.d "Take Action" Tips

benchmarks program to school, state, and national educational program standards

❑ Use the Common Core State Standards to move your library program forward by collaborating with teachers who need support as they teach reading comprehension, higher-level thinking, and inquiry research.

❑ Become the expert in your building on the Common Core State Standards and use AASL's Common Core crosswalks to find where CCSS align with traditional library curriculum.

❑ Consider becoming a National Board Certified Teacher (NBCT) in K–12 Library Media/ Early Childhood through Young Adulthood, the highest certification school librarians can attain.

❑ Plan and assess your school library program using AASL's *Standards for the 21st-Century Learner* and *Empowering Learners: Guidelines for School Library Programs*.

❑ Obtain the state-mandated credentials for becoming a Lead Teacher to help you expand your leadership role in your building.

Action 3.1.e "Take Action" Tips

takes responsibility for professional growth through continuous program improvement

- ❏ Tie your professional development plan and personal learning network activities to the program goals of your library and district.

- ❏ Take your library program goals to training sessions to help you stay on track.

Action 3.1.f "Take Action" Tips

creates an environment that is conducive to active and participatory learning, resource-based learning, and collaboration with teaching staff

- ❏ Use your knowledge of curriculum resources to collaborate with your teachers to create instructional units that are resource-based and student-centered.

- ❏ Focus your collaborative lessons on student talk, interaction with information, and active learning.

- ❏ Bring together resources in multiple formats to support your collaborative lessons to meet the needs of your learners, while designing lessons around your state's adopted standards.

Action 3.1.g "Take Action" Tips

uses research to inform practice and makes evidence-based decisions

- ❏ Base your professional practice and decision-making on the best evidence you can find in the library literature, the evidence you collect locally, and your professional judgment.

- ❏ Strive to both collect and publish your local evidence so that other librarians can also benefit and improve the learning of their students.

Action 3.1.h "Take Action" Tips

is a visible and active leader within the school community

- ❏ Use evidence-based practice to boost your role as a leader in your building and the local school community, and to prove that you are on an equal footing with the other teachers.

- ❏ Share your data collection methods with other teachers one-to-one or in a staff development environment by showing them how to collect data from blogs, tablet computers, and online testing.

- ❏ Make sure the tool your principal uses to evaluate you includes your leadership role.

Action 3.1.i "Take Action" Tips

is an early adopter of changes in current educational and technology trends

- ❏ Cultivate the characteristics of librarians (e.g., interpersonal skills) that make them change agents.

- ❏ Use your love of reading and learning to stay abreast of current research and issues in the field of librarianship, such as formative assessment strategies, social-media learning tools, and one-to-one digital devices for students.

- ❏ Internalize the student-learning standards adopted by your state.

3.1 EMPOWERING LEARNING THROUGH LEADERSHIP: Leadership

Action 3.1.j "Take Action" Tips

My Actions

participates in local, regional, state, and national professional associations for education and librarianship

❏ Join your local, regional, state, and national school library organizations as step 1 in your journey to becoming an Exemplary-level librarian and use the support of colleagues to guide you.

❏ Use your librarianship to become a leader beyond the local level, at the regional, state, and national levels, and make these organizations the core of your personal learning network.

Action 3.1.k "Take Action" Tips

serves on the decision-making team of the school

❏ Volunteer to be a member of your building or district-wide Response to Intervention (RTI) team to help improve student learning.

❏ Join a school team or committee whose purpose is to research a new initiative, such as one-to-one technology, college and career readiness, bring your own device (BYOD), or sustained silent reading (SSR), because your work is that of the whole school.

Action 3.1.l "Take Action" Tips

shares best practices and research by publishing articles in state and national professional journals

❏ Begin your publishing by creating your own website, wiki, blog, or electronic learning-management system page, followed by feature articles in your school newsletter, local newspaper, and your state's school library association publication.

❏ Publish articles in national school library journals such as *Knowledge Quest* and, if you have accumulated significant knowledge in one area of librarianship, author an AASL publication for school library professionals.

COLLECT EVIDENCE

Multiple examples of "Evidence of Accomplishment" are located in the Appendix at the end of this workbook. Review the list of potential evidence and select items that document the work you already do in your library. Brainstorm ways that you can add new evidence to your practice. Enter the action you will be implementing below. Use the "My Evidence of Accomplishment" space to record and organize evidence of your practice that you've already collected or plan to collect. Create a portfolio and share it with your principal during the librarian evaluation process.

ACTION _____

_____ _____

_____

My Evidence of Accomplishment

MY ACTION PLAN KEY:

Goal Type

Short-term
Long-term
Part of Strategic Plan
Professional Development
Leader Role
Instructional Partner Role
Information Specialist Role
Teacher Role
Program Administrator Role

My Target Audience

SCHOOL COMMUNITY:
Students
Teachers
Administrators
Advisory Committee
Planning Committee
Friends of the Library
Volunteers (Student/Adult)

EXTERNAL STAKEHOLDERS:
Parents
Local Community
Business Community
Public Library
Academic Library
State Community
National Community
Global Community

My Professional Development Venue

District In-Service
Local/Regional Conference
State Conference
AASL National Conference
Community Learning
College Course
Evidence Collection
Action Research
Readings

Task Timeline

This Week
This Month
This Grading Period
This Semester
This Year
Next Year
2–3 Year Plan

MY ACTION PLAN

Use the "My Action Plan" worksheet to guide your planning process to accomplish the guideline action. After digesting the readings, noting appropriate action strategies, and entering your evidence information, consider and record your goals, target audience, tasks, timelines, and professional development plans. Enter the action you will be implementing below and use the key in the sidebar to help you complete your plan.

ACTION _____

_____   _____

_____

MY GOAL

Goal Type: _____
My Target Audience: _____

Task 1	Timeline
Task 2	Timeline
Task 3	Timeline

My Professional Development Plan | Venue

MY GOAL

Goal Type: _____
My Target Audience: _____

Task 1	Timeline
Task 2	Timeline
Task 3	Timeline

My Professional Development Plan | Venue

MY GOAL

Goal Type: _____
My Target Audience: _____

Task 1	Timeline
Task 2	Timeline
Task 3	Timeline

My Professional Development Plan | Venue

APPENDICES

APPENDIX A:
School Librarian Evaluation Rubric

Each level of the School Librarian Evaluation Rubric builds on the one before, beginning with foundational and ending with exemplary. The goal of the rubric is to support a librarian's professional growth over time, and therefore the rubric can be regarded as modular. Because each librarian's personal development and state, district, and school environment is unique, librarians can adapt the rubric to suit their needs.

1. TEACHING FOR LEARNING

1.1 BUILDING COLLABORATIVE PARTNERSHIPS:
The school library program promotes collaboration among members of the learning community and encourages learners to be independent, lifelong users and producers of ideas and information.

FOUNDATIONAL	DEVELOPING	MASTERY	EXEMPLARY
The school librarian:	The school librarian:	The school librarian:	The school librarian:
a. collaborates with a core team of classroom teachers and specialists to design, implement, and evaluate inquiry lessons and units.	**b.** collaborates with an extended team that includes parents, members of the community, museums, academic and public libraries, municipal services, private organizations, and commercial entities to include their expertise and assistance in inquiry lessons and units.	**c.** works with administrators to actively promote, support, and implement collaboration.	**d.** seeks input from students on the learning process.

NOTES:

1. TEACHING FOR LEARNING

1.2 THE ROLE OF READING:
The school library program promotes reading as a foundational skill for learning, personal growth, and enjoyment.

FOUNDATIONAL	DEVELOPING	MASTERY	EXEMPLARY
The school librarian:	The school librarian:	The school librarian:	The school librarian:
a. acquires and promotes current, high-quality, high-interest collections of books and other reading resources in multiple formats.	**f.** creates opportunities to involve caregivers, parents, and other family members in reading.	**g.** models reading strategies in formal and informal instruction.	**h.** collaborates with teachers and other specialists to integrate reading strategies into lessons and units of instruction.
b. fosters reading for various pursuits, including personal pleasure, knowledge, and ideas.			
c. creates an environment where independent reading is valued, promoted, and encouraged.			
d. develops initiatives to encourage and engage learners in reading, writing, and listening for understanding and enjoyment.			
e. motivates learners to read fiction and nonfiction through reading aloud, booktalking, displays, exposure to authors, and other means.			

NOTES:

APPENDIX A: School Librarian Evaluation Rubric

1. TEACHING FOR LEARNING

1.3 ADDRESSING MULTIPLE LITERACIES:
The school library program provides instruction that addresses multiple literacies, including information literacy, media literacy, visual literacy, and technology literacy.

FOUNDATIONAL	DEVELOPING	MASTERY	EXEMPLARY
The school librarian:	The school librarian:	The school librarian:	The school librarian:
a. promotes critical thinking by connecting learners with the world of information in multiple formats.	**f.** provides instruction specific to searching for information in various formats.	**h.** encourages the use of multiple formats to present data and information in compelling and useful ways.	**i.** collaborates with classroom teachers to embed skills associated with multiple literacies into lessons and curricular units.
b. stays abreast of emerging technologies and formats.	**g.** adapts to and models new skills, new technologies, and new understandings of the learning process.		
c. integrates the use of state-of-the-art and emerging technologies as a means for effective and creative learning.			
d. guides students and teachers to formats most appropriate for the learning task.			
e. embeds key concepts of legal, ethical and social responsibilities in accessing, using and creating information in various formats.			

NOTES:

APPENDIX A: School Librarian Evaluation Rubric

1. TEACHING FOR LEARNING

1.4 EFFECTIVE PRACTICES FOR INQUIRY:
The school library program models an inquiry-based approach to learning and the information search process.

FOUNDATIONAL	DEVELOPING	MASTERY	EXEMPLARY
The school librarian:	The school librarian:	The school librarian:	The school librarian:
a. supports educational and program standards as defined by the local, state, and national associations.	**c.** adapts to and models new technologies and new understandings of the learning process.	**f.** provides aids that help learners collect information and data.	**i.** stimulates critical thinking through the use of learning activities that involve application, analysis, evaluation, and creativity.
b. integrates the use of state-of-the-art and emerging technologies as a means for effective and creative learning.	**d.** designs learning tasks that incorporate the information search process.	**g.** provides opportunities for learners to revise their work through feedback from educators and peers.	**j.** uses differentiated strategies with respect to gender, reading ability, personal interests, and prior knowledge to engage learners in reading and inquiry.
	e. builds upon learners' prior knowledge as needed for the learning task.	**h.** uses formative assessments to guide learners and assess their progress.	**k.** uses diagnostics, including observation, checklists, and graphic organizers, to identify zones of intervention.
			l. applies appropriate interventions to help learners perform tasks that they cannot complete without assistance.

NOTES:

APPENDIX A: School Librarian Evaluation Rubric

1. TEACHING FOR LEARNING

1.5 ASSESSMENT IN TEACHING FOR LEARNING:
The school library program is guided by regular assessment of student learning to ensure the program is meeting its goals.

FOUNDATIONAL	DEVELOPING	MASTERY	EXEMPLARY
The school librarian:	The school librarian:	The school librarian:	The school librarian:
a. implements critical analysis and evaluation strategies.	**c.** solicits student input for the assessment of inquiry-based instructional units upon their completion.	**e.** uses formative assessments that give students feedback and the chance to revise their work.	**g.** creates rubrics for student work that integrate curricular, informational, and critical thinking standards.
b. uses summative assessments of process and product in collaboration with teachers.	**d.** solicits student input for post-assessment of inquiry-based instructional units.	**f.** uses performance-based assessments, such as rubrics, checklists, portfolios, journals, observation, conferencing, and self-questioning.	**h.** documents student progress through portfolios that demonstrate growth.

NOTES:

2. BUILDING THE LEARNING ENVIRONMENT

2.1 PLANNING AND EVALUATING:
The school library program is built on a long-term strategic plan that reflects the mission, goals, and objectives of the school.

FOUNDATIONAL	DEVELOPING	MASTERY	EXEMPLARY
The school librarian:	The school librarian:	The school librarian:	The school librarian:
a. uses strategic planning for the continuous improvement of the program.	**d.** conducts ongoing evaluation that creates the data needed for strategically planning comprehensive and collaborative long-range goals for program improvement.	**g.** analyzes the data and sets priorities articulated as goals.	**h.** generates evidence in practice that demonstrates the efficacy and relevance of the school library instructional program.
b. develops, with input from the school community, mission statements and goals for the school library program that support the mission, goals, and objectives of the school.	**e.** uses evidence of practice, particularly in terms of learning outcomes, to support program goals and planning.		**i.** uses research findings to inform decision making and teaching practices.
c. writes objectives for each goal that include steps to be taken to attain the goal, a timeline, and a method of determining if the objective was attained.	**f.** uses action research, a tool of evidence-based practice, to provide methods for collection of evidence and input from users through interviews, surveys, observations, journaling, focus groups, content analysis, and statistics.		**j.** plans for the future through data collection, program evaluation, and strategic planning.

NOTES:

2. BUILDING THE LEARNING ENVIRONMENT

2.2 STAFFING:
The school library program has a minimum of one full-time certified/licensed school librarian supported by qualified staff sufficient for the school's instructional programs, services, facilities, size, and number of teachers and students.

FOUNDATIONAL	DEVELOPING	MASTERY	EXEMPLARY
The school librarian:	The school librarian:	The school librarian:	The school librarian:
a. writes job descriptions that outline the roles, responsibilities, competencies, and qualifications of library staff, including paraprofessionals, student aides, and community volunteers. **b.** works in collaboration with each staff member to evaluate job descriptions on a regular basis.	**c.** analyzes the instructional program to determine appropriate staffing patterns. **d.** provides appropriate training and support for student aides and volunteers.	**e.** works with administrators to ensure that the program is adequately staffed with professional and supporting staff.	**f.** creates an environment of mutual respect and collaboration in which all staff members work toward the common goal of student learning.

NOTES:

APPENDIX A: School Librarian Evaluation Rubric

2. BUILDING THE LEARNING ENVIRONMENT

2.3 LEARNING SPACE:
The school library program includes flexible and equitable access to physical and virtual collections of resources that support the school curriculum and meet the diverse needs of all learners.

FOUNDATIONAL	DEVELOPING	MASTERY	EXEMPLARY
The school librarian:	The school librarian:	The school librarian:	The school librarian:
a. ensures that library hours provide optimum access for learners and other members of the school community.	**d.** ensures that technology and telecommunications infrastructure is adequate to support teaching and learning.	**f.** promotes flexible scheduling of the school library facility to allow for efficient and timely integration of resources into the curriculum.	**h.** creates an environment that is conducive to active and participatory learning, resource-based learning, and collaboration with teaching staff.
b. creates a friendly, comfortable, well-lit, aesthetically pleasing, and ergonomic space that is centrally located and well integrated with the rest of the school.	**e.** provides space and seating that enhance and encourage technology use, leisure reading and browsing, and use of materials in all formats.	**g.** designs and maintains a library website that provides 24-7 access to digital information resources, instructional interventions, reference services, links to other libraries and academic sites, information for parents, and exhibits of exemplary student work.	**i.** designs learning spaces that accommodate a range of teaching methods, learning tasks, and learning outcomes.
c. provides sufficient and appropriate shelving and storage of resources.			

NOTES:

2. BUILDING THE LEARNING ENVIRONMENT

2.4 BUDGET:
The school library program has sufficient funding to support priorities and make steady progress to attain the program's mission, goals, and objectives.

FOUNDATIONAL	DEVELOPING	MASTERY	EXEMPLARY
The school librarian:	The school librarian:	The school librarian:	The school librarian:
a. creates a budget that ensures the library is adequately funded to support the program guidelines.	**c.** collects current market data about information resource costs and shares the information with decision makers, such as site councils, administrators, and district financial officers.	**e.** allocates funding through strategic planning to support priorities and make steady progress to attain outlined goals and objectives.	**g.** supports the budget with local and nationally published evidence that shows how the school library program impacts learning.
b. meets regularly with the school principal and/or district chief financial officer to discuss the library budget.	**d.** seeks additional funding through fundraisers, grant writing, and parent donation programs.	**f.** creates budget rationales and priorities using evidence from strategic planning.	

NOTES:

APPENDIX A: School Librarian Evaluation Rubric

2. BUILDING THE LEARNING ENVIRONMENT

2.5 POLICIES:
The school library program includes policies, procedures, and guidelines that support equitable access to ideas and information throughout the school community.

FOUNDATIONAL	DEVELOPING	MASTERY	EXEMPLARY
The school librarian:	The school librarian:	The school librarian:	The school librarian:
a. establishes school library program acquisition, processing, and cataloging procedures that conform with district policies. **b.** establishes policies and procedures for the circulation of library materials.	**c.** establishes policies for reserving and scheduling use of library spaces and resources. **d.** seeks input from appropriate members of the school community when developing policies.	**e.** develops and implements board-approved collection development policies, including those for selection and purchasing. **f.** works with the technology department and school administrators to develop and implement acceptable-use policies. **g.** works in conjunction with other school library professionals in the district to establish a reconsideration policy for challenged materials, which is adopted by the local board of education.	**h.** works with faculty to develop policies that guide the ethical use of information.

NOTES:

2. BUILDING THE LEARNING ENVIRONMENT

2.6 COLLECTION AND INFORMATION ACCESS:
The school library program includes a well-developed collection of books, periodicals, and non-print material in a variety of formats that support curricular topics and are suited to inquiry learning and users' needs and interests.

FOUNDATIONAL	DEVELOPING	MASTERY	EXEMPLARY
The school librarian:	The school librarian:	The school librarian:	The school librarian:
a. advocates for and protects intellectual access to information and ideas.	**d.** ensures the collection is centralized and decentralized as needed to support classroom activities and other learning initiatives in the school.	**g.** collaborates with the teaching staff to develop an up-to-date collection of print and digital resources in multiple genres that appeals to differences in age, gender, ethnicity, reading abilities, and information needs.	**i.** maps the collection to ensure that it meets the needs of the school curriculum.
b. tracks inventory in the school library, taking advantage of up-to-date automation systems and keeping current with software releases and training.	**e.** promotes alternative reading options through readinglists,bibliographies, and webliographies that include periodicals, bestseller lists, graphic novels, books, and websites in multiple languages.	**h.** regularly seeks input from students through such tools as surveys and suggestion boxes to determine students' reading interests and motivations.	**j.** reviews challenged materials using the reconsideration policy.
c. conducts regular weeding to ensure that the library collection is up to date.	**f.** links the digital library to local, regional, or state online networks, connecting with other public or academic libraries to take advantage of available virtual resources to support the school curriculum.		

NOTES:

2. BUILDING THE LEARNING ENVIRONMENT

2.7 OUTREACH:
The school library program is guided by an advocacy plan that builds support from decision makers who affect the quality of the school library program.

FOUNDATIONAL	DEVELOPING	MASTERY	EXEMPLARY
The school librarian:	The school librarian:	The school librarian:	The school librarian:
a. forms a "Friends of the School Library" program.	**f.** communicates to stakeholders through the library website, parent newsletters, e-mail, and other formats.	**h.** builds relationships with local, state, and national decision makers.	**i.** uses local, state, national, and international school library data to engage support.
b. encourages parents and community members to support learners by volunteering in the library.	**g.** offers to provide informational programs for community special-interest and service groups.		**j.** forms partnerships with the local and global community to promote student learning.
c. participates in PTA/ PTO or other school-based parent groups.			**k.** analyzes stakeholder goals and issues for potential alignment with library activities and resources, and builds promotional efforts around them.
d. encourages visits to and use of the library by parents, administrators, elected officials, and other stakeholders.			**l.** writes articles and regular reports giving concrete evidence of what the library does to prepare learners to be successful in the twenty-first century.
e. attends department, curriculum, faculty, and other school- and district-based meetings.			

NOTES:

2. BUILDING THE LEARNING ENVIRONMENT

2.8 PROFESSIONAL DEVELOPMENT:
The school library program includes support for school librarian and teacher professional development to sustain and increase knowledge and skills.

FOUNDATIONAL	DEVELOPING	MASTERY	EXEMPLARY
The school librarian:	The school librarian:	The school librarian:	The school librarian:
a. reads research relevant to school libraries, student learning, and new developments in the educational field.	**b.** ensures access to professional development opportunities for professional and paraprofessional staff.	**d.** participates in and provides professional development to sustain and to develop knowledge and skills.	**f.** participates in local, regional, state, and national educational conferences as a learner and as a teacher.
	c. takes advantage of professional development opportunities and shares new learning with the school administration and faculty.	**e.** seeks opportunities to teach new skills to the faculty and staff, whether in a classroom setting or one-on-one instruction.	

NOTES:

3. EMPOWERING LEARNING THROUGH LEADERSHIP

3.1 LEADERSHIP:
The school library program is built by professionals who model leadership and best practice for the school community.

FOUNDATIONAL	DEVELOPING	MASTERY	EXEMPLARY
The school librarian:	The school librarian:	The school librarian:	The school librarian:
a. shares knowledge about libraries and learning by publishing articles in the school newsletter or other community news sources.	**d.** benchmarks program to school, state, and national educational program standards.	**h.** is a visible and active leader within the school community.	**k.** serves on the decision-making team of the school.
b. shares expertise by presenting information at faculty meetings, parent meetings, and school board meetings.	**e.** takes responsibility for professional growth through continuous program improvement.	**i.** is an early adopter of changes in current educational and technology trends.	**l.** shares best practices and research by publishing articles in state and national professional journals.
c. fosters an atmosphere of respect and rapport between the school librarian and all members of the learning community to encourage student learning and to promote teacher enthusiasm and participation.	**f.** creates an environment that is conducive to active and participatory learning, resource-based learning, and collaboration with teaching staff.	**j.** participates in local, regional, state, and national professional associations for education and librarianship.	
	g. uses research to inform practice and makes evidence-based decisions.		

NOTES:

APPENDIX B:
Summative Conference Form

School Librarian Evaluation Information:

STAFF MEMBER: _____

CURRENT POSITION: _____

LIMITED CONTRACT: _____

CONTINUING CONTRACT: _____

EVALUATOR: _____

PRE-OBSERVATION CONFERENCE DATE: _____

OBSERVATION DATE(S): _____

POST-OBSERVATION CONFERENCE DATE: _____

School Librarian Overall Rating Regarding Components:

_____ FOUNDATIONAL

_____
EVALUATOR'S SIGNATURE   DATE

_____ DEVELOPING

_____ MASTERY

_____
LICENSED/CERTIFIED SCHOOL LIBRARIAN SIGNATURE   DATE

* Signature indicates review of the evaluation. Licensed/Certified staff members may attach a response
to this form to become part of their personnel file. Additional pages may be used if necessary.

_____ EXEMPLARY

APPENDIX B: Summative Conference Form

INSTRUCTIONS

Provide this Summative Conference Form to your principal or evaluator to use at the end of your evaluation process. The evaluator may use the grids to summarize the school librarian's accomplishments and progress for each guideline. Space is provided at the end for overall comments from the evaluator and school librarian on each of the three rubric areas. Personnel information and an overall rating may be recorded on the summative cover sheet.

1. Teaching for Learning

GUIDELINE	FOUNDATIONAL	DEVELOPING	MASTERY	EXEMPLARY
1.1 Building Collaborative Partnerships: *Promotes collaboration among members of the learning community and encourages learners to be independent, lifelong users and producers of ideas and information.*				
1.2 The Role of Reading: *Promotes reading as a foundational skill for learning, personal growth, and enjoyment.*				
1.3 Addressing Multiple Literacies: *Provides instruction that addresses multiple literacies, including information literacy, media literacy, visual literacy, and technology literacy.*				
1.4 Effective Practices for Inquiry: *Models an inquiry-based approach to learning and the information search process.*				
1.5 Assessment in Teaching for Learning: *Assesses student learning regularly to ensure the program is meeting its goals.*				

2. Building the Learning Environment

GUIDELINE	FOUNDATIONAL	DEVELOPING	MASTERY	EXEMPLARY
2.1 Planning and Evaluating the School Library Program: *Helps to develop a long-term strategic plan that reflects the mission, goals, and objectives of the school.*				
2.2 Staffing: *Is part of a staff that includes a minimum of one full-time certified/licensed librarian supported by qualified staff sufficient for the school's instructional programs, services, facilities, size, and number of teachers and students.*				
2.3 Learning Space: *Provides flexible and equitable access to physical and virtual collections of resources that support the school curriculum and meet the diverse needs of all learners.*				
2.4 Budget: *Manages funding sufficient to support priorities and make steady progress to attain the program's mission, goals, and objectives.*				
2.5 Policies: *Develops and uses policies, procedures, and guidelines that support equitable access to ideas and information throughout the school community.*				
2.6 Collection and Information Access: *Selects a well-developed collection of books, periodicals, and non-print material in a variety of formats that support curricular topics and are suited to inquiry learning and users' needs and interests.*				
2.7 Outreach: *Implements an advocacy plan that builds support from decision makers who affect the quality of the school library program.*				
2.8 Professional Development: *Engages in and provides professional development to sustain and increase knowledge and skills.*				

3. Empowering Learning through Leadership

GUIDELINE	FOUNDATIONAL	DEVELOPING	MASTERY	EXEMPLARY
3.1 Leadership: *Models professionalism, leadership, and best practice for the school community.*				

1. TEACHING FOR LEARNING

Evaluator Comments:

School Librarian Comments:

2. BUILDING THE LEARNING ENVIRONMENT

Evaluator Comments:

School Librarian Comments:

3. EMPOWERING LEARNING THROUGH LEADERSHIP

Evaluator Comments:

School Librarian Comments:

APPENDIX C:
Evidence of Accomplishment

A

ACCESS

−−, equal, open, barrier-free

−−, intellectual freedom

ADVOCACY

−−, circulating petitions

−−, legislative testimony

−−, writing press releases

AGENDA

−−, in-service

−−, library staff meeting

−−, library staff training

ASSESSMENT

−−, "I learned" statements

−−, alternative

−−, authentic venues

−−, cell phone & smart devices

−−, citations, works cited pages, & annotated bibliographies

−−, communication log

−−, data driven, data-driven decision making

−−, double-entry journal

−−, exit slips

−−, formative

−−, library program

−−, library's role in state

−−, muddiest point

−−, note-taking sample

−−, one-minute paper

−−, online information-literacy test--national

−−, online rubric generator

−−, performance-based

−−, portfolios

−−, pre- & post-tests

−−, real-world

−−, recorded observation

−−, reflection log

−−, rubrics

−−, student response system (SRS) & "clickers"

−−, student work sample

−−, summative

−−, tablet computers

−−, test retakes

AUTHORSHIP

−−, article in *Knowledge Quest* (AASL)

−−, article in local newspaper

−−, article in professional trade journal

−−, article in School Library Research journal (AASL)

−−, article in school newspaper

−−, article in state school library association journal

−−, e-reader content

−−, parent newsletter

−−, professional textbook, commercial publisher

−−, publish professional textbook with national association (AASL)

AWARD

−−, professional, AASL Awards

−−, professional, other

B

BLOG

−−, librarian's

BOOK

−− award voting

−− club & literature circle

−− talk & book hook

BUDGET

−−, fund-raising

−−, maintenance

C

CATALOGING

−− & social networking, online service

−−, pre-processed

CERTIFICATION

−−, National Board Certified Teacher (NBCT)

CHART

−−, scope & sequence

E

F

CIRCULATION

––, "sick kid" packet

––, family literacy material

––, library automation

––, online public access catalog (OPAC)

––, summer reading

COMMITTEE WORK

––, career and college readiness

––, curriculum

––, instructional & curriculum

COMMITTEE WORK (CONT.)

––, intervention or RTI activities

––, reading literacy & promotion

––, school improvement

––, strategic planning

––, technology

COMMITTEE

––, Friends of the Library

––, library planning

––, parent-teacher organization (PTO)

COMMUNITY

––, alumni outreach

––, library outreach

––, parent outreach

CONFEENCE

––, parent-teacher

EVALUATION PROCESS

––, library program

––, school librarian

EVENT

––, Banned Books Week (ALA)

––, Banned Websites Awareness Day (AASL)

––, book fair

––, brown-bag lunch

––, Drop Everything And Read (D.E.A.R).

––, El día de los niños/ El día de los libros

––, family literacy "read over"

––, general

––, National Library Legislative Day (ALA)

––, National Library Week (ALA)

––, manga club

––, poetry slam

––, Read Across America (Dr. Seuss's birthday)

––, read-alouds

––, Right-to-Read Week (RTR)

––, School Library Month

––, Teen Read Week (TRW)

––, Teen Tech Week (TTW)

EVIDENCE

––, personal learning network (PLN)

––, student photos & clips

FACILITIES

––, computer lab & classroom

––, design

––, information desk

––, learning commons design

––, library centralization

––, mobile furniture

––, mobile shelving

––, planning

––, reading nooks

––, self-checkout

––, signage

––, simultaneous usage of space

––, video production

FEEDBACK

––, administrators

––, board of education

––, focus group

––, needs assessment

––, online microblogging service response

––, online survey service

––, periodic

––, social networking profile service "friend count"

––, student

––, student panel

––, suggestion box

––, survey

G

GRANT

––, applications submitted

––, disaster relief, Beyond Words (AASL)

––, Library Services & Technology Act (LSTA)

––, professional, AASL grants

––, Reading is Fundamental (RIF)

––, received

GUIDE

––, database searching

––, How To & Getting Started

––, online pathfinder

––, online subject

I

IMPACT STUDIES

––, student learning

INTERVENTION

––, response to (RTI)

J

JOB DESCRIPTION

––, adult volunteer

––, Friends of the Library

––, library planning committee

––, paraprofessional

––, student volunteer

L

LEADERSHIP

––, instructional

––, professional association

––, school building & district

LEARNING MANAGEMENT SYSTEM

––, class taught by librarian (ex. Moodle)

LESSON

––, blog

––, Boolean logic

––, collaborative

––, college- and career-ready

––, digital literacy

––, distance learning

––, field trip

––, global disposition

––, information literacy

––, interactive whiteboard

––, media literacy

––, print & online resources evaluation criteria

––, reflective process

––, student orientation

––, subject tagging

––, technological

––, textual literacy

––, virtual literacy

––, Web 2.0 tools

––, wiki

LETTER

––, student to author

––, thank you to library

LIBRARY

–– bulletin board, student-created

–– display, student-created

LIBRARY COLLECTION TOOL

––, online homepage storage service

––, online reader's advisory service

––, online website organizer

––, personalized dashboard publishing service

LIBRARY COLLECTION

––, alignment & analysis

––, analysis

––, diverse, balanced, & multicultural

––, English as a second language (ESL)

––, foreign languages

––, free or fee-based electronic databases

––, large-print materials

––, mapping & analysis tool

––, range of ability & levels

LIBRARY POSTERS

––, informational

––, literature-based

LIBRARY TRAINING

––, Friends of the Library volunteers

––, Advisory Committee

––, paraprofessional

––, Planning Committee

––, student volunteers

LINK TO

––, college online public access catalog (OPAC)

––, free online state-created career & college resources

––, homework help at public library

––, public library's online public access catalog (OPAC)

––, websites

LIST

––, audiobook, preloaded audio & video player, portable media player (mp3)

––, book award winners

––, common library vocabulary

––, e-reader, tablet computer

––, interactive e-book

––, local expert & speakers bureau

––, new acquisitions

––, online public access catalog section, "popular reads of your students"

––, reading

––, webliographies, webquests

LOG

––, collaboration

––, communication

––, e-mail

M

MANUAL

––, library policy & procedure

MATERIALS SELECTION

––, student input

MEDIA STORAGE

–– & collaborative service (voice, text, music, podcasts, photographs, and videos)

MEMBERSHIP

––, American Association of School Librarians (AASL)

––, American Library Association (ALA)

––, library consortium

––, parent-teacher organization (PTO)

––, professional association

––, regional library system

––, state library association

MODELING

––, information literacy

O

OPEN HOUSE

––, library

––, school building

P

PARTNERSHIP

––, academic library

––, historical society

––, Information Technology (IT) department

––, legislative

––, local business

––, public library

PERFORMANCE EVALUATION

–– form, school librarian--goal setting

–– form, school librarian--rubric

–– process, library staff

PHONE

––, introductory calls to parents

––, polls

POLICY

––, academic integrity

––, confidentiality

––, copyright

––, cyber safety & acceptable use (AUP)

––, donation

––, ethics

––, intellectual freedom

––, inventory

––, library collection development

––, materials selection

––, privacy

––, reconsideration

––, weeding & deselection

C APPENDIX C: Evidence of Accomplishment

PRESENTATION

––, board of education

––, national library conference

––, stakeholder organizations

––, state library conference

––, students in library

PRODUCTS

––, student-created

PROFESSIONAL DEVELOPMENT

––, association journal, *Knowledge Quest* (AASL)

––, Fall Forum (AASL)

––, librarian recertification

––, National Conference (AASL)

––, professional trade journals

––, state conference

––, webinar

PROGRAM GUIDELINES

––, Empowering Learners (AASL)

PROGRAM PLANNING

––, action research process

––, annual report

––, assessment/evaluation, collaborative

––, goals & objectives

––, library planning committee

––, marketing plan

––, strategic plan, with mission & vision statement

PROMOTIONAL MATERIAL

––, ALA "READ" posters of students & staff

––, contest & game

––, reading

PROMOTIONAL TOOL

––, public service announcement (PSA)

––, school building announcement

––, social networking & microblogging

PUBLIC LIBRARY

––, interlibrary loans

––, instructional collaboration

PURCHASING

––, competitive

R

REFLECTIVE PROCESS

––, school librarian's

RESOURCE SHARING

––, via union catalog

––, with college library

––, with public library

REWARDS

––, bookmark, prize, coupon

S

SCHEDULING

––, fixed

––, flexible

––, reservation system

SCHOOL DISTRICT INITIATIVE

––, bring your own device, (BYOD)

––, college- and career-readiness

––, face-to-face and/or virtual participation

––, sustained silent reading (SSR)

SOCIAL NETWORKING

–– profile service, librarian's page

SOFTWARE

––, library automation

STAFF DEVELOPMENT

––, emerging technologies

––, one-on-one

––, one-shots

––, tutorial

––, webinar

STANDARDS

––, Common Core State Standards (CCSS)

––, Partnership for 21st Century Skills (P21 Framework)

––, *Standards for the 21st-Century Learner* (AASL)

––, state academic content

STATISTICS

––, audiobook, preloaded audio & video player, portable media player (mp3)

––, circulation

––, data collection

––, e-book downloads

––, e-reader, tablet computers

––, free online plagiarism & citation checker

––, interlibrary loan

––, learning commons usage

––, online book reviews

––, program assessment

STUDENT PRODUCT

––, blog

––, book review

––, cartoon & art

––, contest entry

––, gallery walk

––, graphic organizer

––, inquiry-research-based project

––, interview

––, invention

––, microblogging response

––, model or game

––, note-taking sample

––, oral presentation

––, recipe

––, rubric or checklist

––, slide show or slide show presentation

––, social networking profile page

––, speech or debate

––, spreadsheet

––, statistics

––, tag or word cloud

––, timeline

––, video or video clip creation

––, website

––, wiki

––, writing contest

SUPPLIES

supplies, student stations

T

TEACHING

––, adult education

––, blended course

––, college adjunct

––, community college

––, evidence-based practice

––, online college course

––, PSEO course

TEACHING STRATEGY

––, active learning

––, Bloom's Taxonomy

––, brain teasers

––, brainstorming

––, chunking

––, fish bowl

––, free writing

––, graphic organizer

––, guided practice

––, guided questions

––, independent practice

––, independent study

––, inquiry method

––, intervention (RTI)

––, K-W-L

––, learning styles

––, manipulatives

––, mind maps

––, multiple intelligences

––, one-on-one

––, online educational video sharing service

––, optical illusions

––, peer evaluation

––, predicting

––, activating prior knowledge

––, problem solving

––, reading aloud

––, reading log

––, read-write-think

––, scaffolding

––, self-evaluation

––, show don't tell

––, simulations

––, small group

––, streaming video

––, student-centered

––, team building

––, think-pair-share

––, webquest

––, word wall

APPENDIX C: Evidence of Accomplishment

TEACHING TOOL

−−, Best Websites for Teaching and Learning (AASL)

−−, collaboration generator

−−, free online diagram generator

−−, free online plagiarism & citation checker service

−−, free online brainstorming service

−−, free online electronic calendar service

−−, free online gaming service

−−, free online interactive graphic organizer

−−, free online mind mapping tool

−−, free online office suite & data storage service

−−, free online personal homepage storage service

−−, free online social networking service

−−, free online spreadsheet storage service

−−, free online video-editing service

−−, free online website authoring & storage service

−−, free web-based computer-to-computer telephone calling service

−−, interactive whiteboard

−−, online notice board generator

−−, online timeline generator

−−, primary & secondary documents

−−, projector

−−, research calculator

−−, word processing summarizing feature

TECHNOLOGY

−−, assistive & adaptive

−−, copier

−−, e-readers

−−, laptop & netbook

−−, photo & video-editing

−−, scanner

−−, sound system

−−, tablet computers

−−, television

TESTIMONIAL

−−, community member

−−, parent

−−, principal

−−, teacher

TUTORIAL

−−, online educational video-sharing service

−−, college- and career-ready

V

VISIT

−−, author, storyteller, magician, or puppeteer

−−, class accompanied by teacher

−−, college librarian

−−, community guest

−−, public librarian

VOLUNTEER

−−, adult

−−, student

W

WEBSITE

−−, school librarian's

−−, librarian's companion course

WIKI

−−, librarian's

WORKSHOP

−−, community--college, college finances & careers

−−, community--cyber safety

−−, community--homework

−−, community--literacy

−−, community--parents

−−, community--social media

My Evidence of Accomplishment Notes

APPENDIX D:
Additional Suggested Reading

CONTINUED FROM PAGE 21

1.1 TEACHING FOR LEARNING:
Building Collaborative
Partnerships

Stafford, T. 2011. "Analyzing the Cognitive Skills and Inquiry." *School Library Monthly* 28 (2): 8–10.

Wallace, V. L, and W. N. Husid. 2011. *Collaborating for Inquiry-Based Learning: School Librarians and Teachers Partner for Student Achievement.* Santa Barbara, CA: Libraries Unlimited.

CONTINUED FROM PAGE 26

1.2 TEACHING FOR LEARNING:
Role of Reading

Fontichiaro, K. 2011. "Nudging toward Inquiry: Extracting Relevant Information and Note Taking." *School Library Monthly* 27 (4): 12–13.

Friese, B. 2010. "A Collection of Mentors: How the Library Program Can Support Writing Instruction." *School Library Monthly* 26 (7): 17–19.

Gordin, C., and C. Messenger. 2012. "Supporting Emerging Literacy with Free Choice." *School Library Monthly* 28 (5): 16–19.

Harland, P. C. 2011. *Learning Commons: Seven Simple Steps to Transform Your Library.* Santa Barbara, CA: Libraries Unlimited.

Johnson, M. 2012. "Every Student's Reading Teacher: The School Librarian." *School Library Monthly* 28 (5): 27–28.

Johnson, M. J. 2011. "Changing Spaces for Expository Reading." *School Library Monthly* 28 (3): 26–27.

Keller, C. 2012. "Storytelling? Everyone Has a Story." *School Library Monthly* 28 (5): 10–12.

Knowles, E., and M. Smith. 1997. *Reading Connection: Bringing Parents, Teachers, and Librarians Togethe*r. Englewood, CO: Libraries Unlimited.

Knowles, L. 2009. *Differentiated Reading Instruction through Children's Literature.* Santa Barbara, CA: Libraries Unlimited.

Kuta, K. W. 2008. *Reading and Writing to Learn: Strategies across the Curriculum.* Westport, CT: Libraries Unlimited.

Loertscher, D. V., C. Koechlin, S. Zwaan. 2011. *The New Learning Commons Where Learners Win! Reinventing School Libraries and Computer Labs*. Salt Lake City: Hi Willow Research & Publishing.

McGuire, B. 2009. *Active Reading: Activities for Librarians and Teachers*. Westport, CT: Libraries Unlimited.

McPherson, K. 2007. "Teacher-Librarians as Reading Guides." *Teacher Librarian* 35 (2): 70–73.

Messner, P. A., and B. S. Copeland. 2009. *Every Day Reading Incentives*. Westport, CT: Libraries Unlimited.

Nesi, O. 2010. "It's All About Text Appeal." *School Library Journal* 56 (8): 40–42.

Pitcher, S., and B. Mackey. 2004. *Collaborating for Real Literacy: Librarian, Teacher, and Principal*. Worthington, OH: Linworth.

Prenger, K. V. 2008. "Impact of Online Student-Generated Book Reviews on Library Circulation." Diss. University of Central Missouri. UMI: 1460635.

Soltan, R. 2006. *Reading Raps: A Book Club Guide for Librarians, Kids, and Families*. Westport, CT: Libraries Unlimited.

———. 2010. *Solving the Reading Riddle: The Librarian's Guide to Reading Instruction*. Santa Barbara, CA: Libraries Unlimited.

Tilley, C. L. 2009. "Reading Motivation and Engagement." *School Library Monthly* 26 (4): 39–42.

Walker, C., and S. Shaw. 2004. *Teaching Reading Strategies in the School Library*. Westport, CT: Libraries Unlimited.

CONTINUED FROM PAGE 32

1.3 TEACHING FOR LEARNING: Addressing Multiple Literacies

Gabel, D. 2007. "Blogs, Wikis, Websites—How to Research on the Internet." *School Library Monthly* 24 (3): 11–13.

Heaser, C. 2010. "Workable Video Projects." *School Library Monthly* 26 (7): 20–21.

Jansen, B. A. 1995. "Authentic Products: The Motivating Factor in Library Research Projects." *School Library Monthly* 12 (4): 26–27.

Kapular, D. 2012. "Top 100 Sites of 2011." *TL Advisor Blog*. <www.techlearning.com/Default.aspx?tabid=67&EntryId=3467> (accessed March 8, 2012).

Kenney, B. 2011. "Things Are Changing. Fast." *School Library Journal* 57 (5): 28–33.

Kenny, R. 2004. *Teaching TV Production in a Digital World: Integrating Media Literacy*. Westport, CT: Libraries Unlimited.

Kincheloe, J. L., and D. Weil, eds. 2004. *Critical Thinking and Learning: An Encyclopedia for Parents and Teachers*. Westport, CT: Greenwood.

Kranich, N. 2007. "Librarians and Teen Privacy in the Age of Social Networking." *Knowledge Quest* 36 (2): 34–37.

Magiera, J. 2012. "Redefining Instruction with Technology: Five Essential Steps." *Education Week: Teacher*. <www.edweek.org/tm/articles/2012/01/25/tln_magiera1.html> (accessed May 19, 2012).

Mann, S. 2011. "21st-Century School Librarians: Envisioning the Future. School Library Monthly" 28 (2): 29–30.

CONTINUED FROM PAGE 39

1.4 TEACHING FOR LEARNING: Effective Practices for Inquiry

Matteson, A. 2010. "Tweacher (n): The Twitter Enhanced Teacher." *School Library Monthly* 27 (1): 22–23.

McLaren, G. 2011. *The Beginner's Guide to e-Books.* Christchurch, New Zealand: Altavado Ltd.

Nevin, R., M. Nelson, and D. V. Loertscher. 2010. *Google Apps for Education: Building Knowledge in a Safe and Free Environment.* Salt Lake City: Hi Willow Research & Publishing.

Safford, B. 2006. "How to Help Students Handle the Information Overload." *School Library Monthly* 23 (2): 33–34.

Sheneman, L. 2010. "Digital Storytelling: How to Get the Best Results." *School Library Monthly* 27 (1): 40–42.

Summers, S. L. 2005. *Get Them Thinking: Using Media Literacy to Prepare Students for State Assessments.* Worthington, OH: Linworth.

Tishman, S., and A. G. Andrade. 1997. *Critical Squares: Games of Critical Thinking and Understanding.* Englewood, CO: Teacher Ideas Press.

Thomas, M. J. K. 2008. *Re-Designing the High School Library for the Forgotten Half: The Information Needs of Non-College Bound Students.* Westport, CT: Libraries Unlimited.

Williams, R. T., and D. V. Loertscher. 2008. *In Command! Kids and Teens Build and Manage Their Own Information Spaces, and Learning to Manage Themselves in Those Spaces.* Salt Lake City: Hi Willow Research & Publishing.

Downey, A., L. Ramin, and G. Byerly. 2008. "Simple Ways to Add Active Learning to Your Library Instruction." *Texas Library Journal 84* (2): 52–54.

"Easy Ways to Differentiate with Graphic Organizers." 2009. <www.slideshare.net/ulamb/using-graphic-organizers-to-differentiate-instruction> (accessed May 21, 2012).

Education Planet. 2012. "Data Collection Lesson Plans." <www.lessonplanet.com/search?keywords=data+collection&media=lesson> (accessed March 10, 2012).

Fontichiaro, K. 2011. "Nudging toward Inquiry: Common Core Standards." *School Library Monthly* 28 (1): 49–50.

———. 2011. "Nudging toward Inquiry: Formative Assessment." *School Library Monthly* 27 (6): 11–12.

Fredrick, K. 2012. "Keep It in Mind: Tracking Work, Thoughts, Ideas." *School Library Monthly* 28 (4): 23–24.

George Lucas Educational Foundation. 2012. "Classroom Guide: Top Ten Tips for Teaching with New Media." 2012. <www.edutopia.org/ten-tips-teaching-new-media-resource-guide> (accessed March 18, 2012).

———. "Six Tips for Brain-Based Learning." 2012. <www.edutopia.org/brain-based-learning-strategies-resource-guide> (accessed March 18, 2012).

Harker, C., and D. Putonti. 2008. *Library Research with Emergent Readers: Meeting Standards through Collaboration.* Columbus, OH: Linworth.

Herring, J. 2011. "Assumptions, Information Literacy and Transfer in High Schools." *Teacher Librarian* 38 (3): 32–36.

Hoover, D. 2010. "Librarian's Role in the 'Response to Intervention' Model." *Learning & Media* 38 (3): 15.

Intervention Central. n.d. "Response to intervention." <www.interventioncentral.org> (accessed May 21, 2012).

Kachka, A. 2009. "Differentiating Instruction in the Library Media Center." *School Library Media Activities Monthly* 25 (5): 20–21.

Knowles, L. 2009. *Differentiated Instruction through Children's Literature.* Santa Barbara, CA: Libraries Unlimited.

Koechlin, C., and S. Zwaan. 2007. "Everyone Wins: Differentiation in the School Library." <www.ssla.ca/medium_articles/submissions/pdf/winter2008_pdf/everyone_wins_nov282008_ckoechlinandszwaan.pdf> (accessed May 21, 2012).

———. 2008. "Everyone Wins: Differentiation in the School Library." *Teacher Librarian* 35 (5): 8–13.

Kramer, P. K. 2011. "Common Core and School Librarians: An Interview with Joyce Karon." *School Library Monthly* 28 (1): 8–10.

Kuhlthau, C. C. 2004. *Seeking Meaning: A Process Approach to Library and Information Services.* Westport, CT: Libraries Unlimited.

Larsen, K. 2004. "Sink or Swim: Differentiated Instruction in the Library." *Library Media Connection* 23 (3): 14–16.

Lipson, M. Y., and K. K. Wixson. 2010. *Successful Approaches to RTI: Collaborative Practices for Improving K–12 Literacy.* Newark, DE: International Reading Association.

Marzano, R. J. 2010. *Formative Assessment and Standards-Based Grading.* Bloomington, IN: Marzano Research Laboratory.

McPherson, K. 2006. *Writing More Life into the School Library.* <www.redorbit.com/news/education/397059/writing_more_life_into_the_school_library> (accessed May 22, 2012).

Purcell, M.A. 2012. *The Networked Library: A Guide for Educational Use of Social Networking Sites.* Santa Barbara, CA: Linworth.

"Response to Intervention." 2011. *School Library Monthly* 28 (3): 28.

School Library Monthly Blog. 2012. <http://blog.schoollibrarymedia.com> (access May 22, 2012).

Shrock, K. 2012. "Bloomin' Apps: Google Apps to Support Bloom's Revised Taxonomy." <www.schrockguide.net/bloomin-apps.html> (accessed May 22, 2012).

"Standards for the 21st-Century Learner Lesson Plan Database." 2012. <www.ala.org/aasl/guidelinesandstandards/lessonplandatabase/lessonplandb> (accessed March 18, 2012).

State of Washington Office of Public Instruction. n.d. "Response to Intervention." <www.k12.wa.us/RTI /default.aspx> (accessed May 22, 2012).

APPENDIX D: Additional Suggested Reading

Thomas, N. C. 2000. "A Multiplicity of (Research) Models: Alternative Strategies for Diverse Learners." *School Library Monthly* 17 (1): 25–26, 51.

Thomas, N. P. 2011. *Information Literacy and Information Skills Instruction: Applying Research to Practice in the 21st Century School Library*, 3rd ed. Santa Barbara, CA: Libraries Unlimited.

Vanderbilt, K. L. 2005. "Connecting Learning: Brain-Based Strategies for Linking Prior Knowledge in the Library Media Center." *School Library Monthly* 21 (7): 21–23.

Wesson, C. L., and M. J. Keefe. 1995. *Serving Special Needs Students in the School Library Media Center*. Westport, CT: Greenwood.

Wisconsin Educational Communications Board. 2012. "Into the Book: Strategies for Learning." <http://reading.ecb.org/teacher/strategies.html> (accessed May 22, 2012).

Yoshina, J. M., and V. H. Harada. 2007. "Involving Students in Learning through Rubrics." *Library Media Connection* 25 (5): 10–14.

CONTINUED FROM PAGE 46

1.5 TEACHING FOR LEARNING: Assessment in Teaching for Learning)

Harada, V. H., and J. M. Yoshima. 2005. *Assessing Learning: Librarians and Teachers as Partners*. Westport, CT: Libraries Unlimited.

Heard, G. 2002. *The Revision Toolbox: Teaching Techniques that Work*. Portsmouth, NH: Heinemann.

Marcoux, E. 2011. "Turning the Standards toward the Student—A Metacognition Aspect." *Teacher Librarian* 38 (3): 67–68.

Marriott, C. 2006. "Assessing Student Learning in the School Library Media Center: AASL's 2006 Fall Forum." *Knowledge Quest* 34 (5): 49–52.

Miller, A. 2012. "Tame the Beast: Tips For Designing and Using Rubrics." <www.edutopia.org/blog/designing-using-rubrics-andrew-miller> (accessed March 18, 2012).

Purcell, M. 2011. "Digital Portfolio Assessment." *School Library Monthly* 27 (6): 2.

———. 2011. "Digital Portfolios: A Valuable Teaching Tool." *School Library Monthly* 27 (6): 21–22.

Rash, A. M. n.d. "Student-Created Problems Demonstrate Knowledge and Understanding." <www.maa.org/saum/maanotes49/106.html> (March 11, 2012).

Reeves, D. ed. 2007. *Ahead of the Curve: The Power of Assessment to Transform Teaching and Learning*. Bloomington, IN: Solution Tree.

Schrock, K. 2012. "Kathy Schrock's Guide for Educators: Teacher Helpers: Assessment & Rubric Information." <http://school.discoveryeducation.com/schrockguide/assess.html> (accessed May 23, 2012).

D APPENDIX D: Additional Suggested Reading

CONTINUED FROM PAGE 52

2.1 BUILDING THE LEARNING ENVIRONMENT:
Planning and Evaluating

———. 2004. "A Data Mining Primer and Implications for School Library Media Specialists." *Knowledge Quest* 32 (5): 32–35.

Kaaland, C. 2011. "Creating a Districtwide Advocacy Plan, Part 1: Vision and Voice." *School Library Monthly* 28 (3): 29–31.

———. 2012. "Creating a Districtwide Advocacy Plan, Part 2: Visibility and Vigilance." *School Library Monthly* 28 (4): 29–31.

Langhorne, M. 2005. "Evidence-Based Practice: Show Me the Evidence! Using Data in Support of Library Media Programs." *Knowledge Quest* 33 (5): 35–37.

Library Research Service. 2012. "School Library Information."<www.lrs.org/school> (accessed May 24, 2012).

Martin, A. M. 2011. "Data-Driven Leadership." *School Library Monthly* 28 (2): 31–33.

Matthews, S. 2010. "21st Century Library Strategic Plan—Mission Statement." *21st Century Library Blog* (July 8). <http://21stcenturylibrary. com/2010/07/08/21st-century-library-strategic-plan-%e2%80%93-mission-statement> (accessed May 24, 2012).

——— "21st Century Library Strategic Plan—Vision Statement." *21st Century Library Blog* (July 15). <http://21stcenturylibrary. com/2010/07/15/21st-century-library-strategic-plan-%e2%80%93-vision-statement> (accessed May 24, 2012).

Ohio Educational Library Media Associations. n.d. "Articles and Books about Evidence-Based Practice." <www. oelma.org/EBPBiblio.htm> (accessed May 24, 2012).

Pappas, M. L. 2004. "Planning Goals and Time." *School Library Media Activities Monthly* 21 (1): 40–41.

———. 2008. "Designing Learning for Evidence-Based Practice." *School Library Media Activities Monthly* 24 (5): 20–23.

Snyder, M. M., and J. Roche. 2008. "Road Map for Improvement: Evaluating Your Library Media Program." *Knowledge Quest* 37 (2): 22–27.

Sykes, J. A. 2002. *Action Research: A Practical Guide for Transforming Your School Library*. Greenwood, CO: Libraries Unlimited.

Todd, R. J. 2008. "Evidence-Based Manifesto for School Librarians." *School Library Journal* 54 (4): 38–43.

———. 2009. "School Librarianship and Evidence Based Practice: Progress, Perspectives, and Challenges." *Evidence Based Library and Information Practice* 4 (2): 78–96.

———. 2011. "Charting Student Learning through Inquiry." *School Library Monthly* 28 (3): 5–8.

Yukawa, J., and V. H. Harada. 2009. "Librarian-Teacher Partnerships for Inquiry Learning: Measures of Effectiveness for a Practice-Based Model of Professional Development." *Evidence Based Library and Information Practice* 4 (2): 97–119.

Zilonis, M. F., C. Markuson, and M. B. Fincke. 2002. *Strategic Planning for School Library Media Centers*. Lanham, MD: Scarecrow.

D APPENDIX D: Additional Suggested Reading

CONTINUED FROM PAGE 58

2.2 BUILDING THE LEARNING ENVIRONMENT: Staffing

Morris, B. J. 2010. *Administering the School Library Media Center*. Santa Barbara, CA: Libraries Unlimited.

National Board for Professional Teaching Standards. 2007. *NBPTS Library Media Standards for Teachers of Students Ages 3–18+*. <www.nbpts.org/userfiles/File/ecya_lm_standards.pdf> (accessed March 7, 2012).

Owen, P. L. 2011. "An Improved 'Form of Our Own' A 21st Century Approach to School Librarian Evaluation." *Library Media Connection* 30 (3): 30–33.

Taracuk, K. 2009. "Tips for Administrators: From a Librarian's Point of View." *Ohio Media Spectrum* 61 (1): 19–22.

Wilson, P. P., and J. A. Lyders. 2001. *Leadership for Today's School Library: A Handbook for the Library Media Specialist and the School Principal*. Westport, CT: Greenwood.

CONTINUED FROM PAGE 63

2.3 BUILDING THE LEARNING ENVIRONMENT: Learning Space

Loertscher, D. V., C. Koechlin, and S. Zwaan. 2011. *The New Learning Commons Where Learners Win!: Reinventing School Libraries and Computer Labs*, 2nd ed. Spring, TX: Hi Willow Research & Publishing.

Loertscher, D., and C. Koechlin. 2011. "The School Learning Commons Knowledge Building Center." <https://sites.google.com/site/schoollearningcommons> (accessed March 10, 2012).

Marcoux, Elizabeth. 2009. "The 10-Week Memo and Technology." *Teacher Librarian* 37 (2): 82–83.

Martin, A. M., D. D. Westmoreland, and A. Branyon. 2011. "New Design Considerations That Transform the Library into an Indispensable Learning Environment." *Teacher Librarian* 38 (5): 15–20.

Matthews, J. R. 2004. *Technology Planning: Preparing and Updating a Library Technology Plan*. Westport, CT: Libraries Unlimited.

McGregor, J. H. 2002. "Flexible Scheduling: How Does a Principal Facilitate implementation?" *School Libraries Worldwide* 8 (1): 71–84.

Morris, B. J. 2010. *Administering the School Library Media Center*, 5th ed. Santa Barbara, CA: Libraries Unlimited.

November, A., C. Staudt, M. A. Costello, and L. Huske. 1998. "Critical Issue: Developing a School or District Technology Plan." <www.ncrel.org/sdrs/areas/issues/methods/technlgy/te300.htm> (accessed March 10, 2012).

Ohio Educational Library Media Association. 2007. "Library Media Center Recommendations for the Ohio School Design Manual." <www.oelma.org/advocacy/Library%20Media%20Center%20Recommendations.pdf> (accessed March 10, 2012).

Sargeant, C., and R. Nevin. 2008. "Using the Library Learning Commons to Reengage Disengaged Students and Making it a Student-Friendly Place for Everyone." *Teacher Librarian* 36 (1): 43–45.

Stephens, C. G., and P. Franklin. 2007. *Library 101: A Handbook for the School Library Media Specialist*. Westport, CT: Libraries Unlimited.

Stolley, K. 2011. *How to Design and Write Web Pages Today*. Santa Barbara, CA: Greenwood.

Valenza, J. 2011. "Fully Loaded: Outfitting a Teacher Librarian for the 21st Century. Here's What It Takes." *School Library Journal* 57 (1): 36–38.

Walbert, D. 2011. "Best Practices in School Library Website Design." <www.learnnc.org/lp/pages/969> (accessed March 10, 2012).

Waskow, L. M. 2011. "The Journey from Library Media Center to Learning Commons." *Teacher Librarian* 38 (5): 8–14.

Woolls, B. 2008. *The School Library Media Manager*, 4th ed. Westport, CT: Libraries Unlimited.

CONTINUED FROM PAGE 69

2.4 BUILDING THE LEARNING ENVIRONMENT: Budget

Repman, J., and G. K. Dickinson, eds. 2007. *School Library Management*, 6th ed. Columbus, OH: Linworth.

Small, R. V., and J. Snyder. 2010. "Research Instruments for Measuring the Impact of School Libraries on Student Achievement and Motivation." *School Libraries Worldwide* 16 (1): 61–72.

Staines, G. M. 2011. *Go Get That Grant!: A Practical Guide for Libraries and Nonprofit Organizations*. Lanham, MD: Scarecrow.

Stephens, C. G., and P. Franklin. 2007. *Library 101: A Handbook for the School Library Media Specialist*. Westport, CT: Libraries Unlimited.

United States Department of Education. 2010. "Improving Literacy through School Libraries." <www2.ed.gov/programs/lsl/index.html> (accessed March 11, 2012).

APPENDIX D: Additional Suggested Reading

CONTINUED FROM PAGE 74

2.5 BUILDING THE LEARNING ENVIRONMENT: Policies

Baule, S. M., and J. E. Lewis. 2012. *Social Networking for Schools.* Santa Barbara, CA: Linworth.

Bishop, K. 2007. *The Collection Program in Schools: Concepts, Practices, and Information Sources*, 4th ed. Westport, CT: Libraries Unlimited.

Buzzeo, T. 2008. *The Collaboration Handbook.* Columbus, OH: Linworth.

Crowley, J. D. 2011. *Developing Visions: Strategic Planning for the School Librarian in the 21st century*, 2nd ed. Santa Barbara, CA: Libraries Unlimited.

Dow, M. 2008. "Teaching Ethical Behavior in the Global World of Information and the New AASL Standards." *School Library Media Activities Monthly* 25 (4): 49–52.

Dylan, J., producer. 2011. *A Shared Culture: Creative Commons.* <http://creativecommons.org/videos/a-shared-culture> (accessed March 13, 2012).

Franklin, P., and C. G. Stephens. 2007. "Cataloging and Processing: Getting It on the Shelf So It Can Go Out the Door!" *School Library Media Activities Monthly* 23 (8): 48–50.

Gustafson, C. 2010. "When There's a Closed Sign on the Library Door." *Library Media Connection* 29 (3): 20.

Hill, R. 2010. "The Problem of Self-Censorship." *School Library Monthly* 27 (2): 9–12.

Hurley, C. A. 2004. "Fixed vs. Flexible Scheduling in School Library Media Centers: A Continuing Debate." *Library Media Connection* 23 (3): 36–41.

Kachka, A. 2012. "Lexile Level Analysis as a Collection Development Tool." *School Library Monthly* 28 (4): 35–36.

Kaplan, A. G., and A. M. Riedling. 2006. *Catalog It!: A Guide to Cataloging School Library Materials.* Worthington, OH: Linworth.

Lamb, A. 2010. "Everyone Does It: Teaching Ethical Use of Social Technology." *Knowledge Quest* 39 (1): 62–67.

LaPierriere, J., and T. Christiansen. 2008. *Merchandising Made Simple: Using Standards and Dynamite Displays to Boost Circulation.* Westport, CT: Libraries Unlimited.

Maycock, A. 2011. "Issues and Trends in Intellectual Freedom for Teacher Librarians." *Teacher Librarian* 39 (1): 8–12.

Miller, P. 2004. "Getting Around." *School Library Media Activities Monthly* 20 (7): 44, 47.

Pappas, M. L. 2004. "Selection Policies." *School Library Media Activities Monthly* 21 (2): 41, 45.

Preer, J. 2008. *Library Ethics.* Westport, CT: Libraries Unlimited.

Scales, P. 2010. "Every Breath You Take." *School Library Journal* 56 (11): 19.

Scheeren, W. O. 2012. *The Hidden Web: A Sourcebook.* Santa Barbara, CA: Libraries Unlimited.

Shaw, M. K. 1999. *Block Scheduling and Its Impact on the School Library Media Center.* Westport, CT: Greenwood Press.

Von Drasek, L. 2007. "It Begins with a Question: Meeting with a Parent." *Knowledge Quest* 36 (2): 66–68.

CONTINUED FROM PAGE 80

2.6 BUILDING THE LEARNING ENVIRONMENT: Collection and Information Access

Bailey, K. 2011. "Efficient Solutions for Time-Consuming Jobs in the Library." *Computers in Libraries* 31 (9): 32–35.

Baumbach, D. J., and L. L. Miller. 2006. *Less is More: a Practical Guide to Weeding School Library Collections.* Chicago: ALA.

Braxton, B. 2004. "Putting Your School Library Online." *Teacher Librarian* 31 (4): 52–53.

Callison, D. 1998. "Student-Talk." *School Library Media Activities Monthly* 14 (10): 38–41.

Center for Children's Books, Graduate School of Library and Information Science, University of Illinois at Urbana-Champaign. 2003. "What to Do When a Book Is Being Challenged in Your Library." <http://ccb.lis.illinois.edu/challenge.html> (accessed March 13, 2012).

Dearman, M., and E. Dumas. 2008. "Weeding and Collection Development Go Hand-in-Hand." *Louisiana Libraries* 71 (2): 11–14.

Fitzgibbons, S. A. 2004. "What Motivates Reading? How Library Media Specialists Can Contribute to the Development of Good Readers." *School Library Monthly* 20 (10): 21–25, 35.

Foote, C. 2010. "Putting Your Best Foot Forward." *School Library Journal* 56 (1): 40–42.

Franklin, P., and C. G. Stephens. 2007. "Creating Web Pages for the 21st Century Media Center." *School Library Media Activities Monthly* 24 (3): 41–42.

Fuller, D. 2006. "2006 Automation Survey." *School Library Journal* 52 (10): 48–52.

Howard, J. K. 2010. "Information Specialist and Leader—Taking on Collection and Curriculum Mapping." *School Library Monthly* 27 (1): 35–37.

———. 2011. "Basic Selection Tools: 21st-Century Style." *School Library Monthly* 28 (3): 9–11.

Johns, S. K. 2007. "Who's Protecting Whom? AASL and Intellectual Freedom." *Knowledge Quest* 36 (2): 4–6.

Kachka, A. 2012. "Lexile Level Analysis as a Collection Development Tool." *School Library Monthly* 28 (4): 35–36.

Loertscher, D. 2007. "Children, Teens, and the Construction of Information Spaces." *Teacher Librarian* 35 (2): 14–17.

Marcoux, E. 2009. "Intellectual Access to Information: The Teacher-Librarian as Facilitator." *Teacher Librarian* 36 (5): 76–77.

———. 2011. "Chapter One: The Start of the Learning Commons Approach." *Teacher Librarian* 39 (2): 16–21.

McKenzie, D. 2011. "Digital Resourcing and Access in the School Library: A Pandora's Box of Problems, Ponderings, and Potential." *Library Media Connection* 29 (4): 56–57.

Sanacore, J. 2006. "Teacher-Librarians, Teachers, and Children as Cobuilders of School Library Collections." *Teacher Librarian* 33 (5): 24–29.

Schwelik, J. C., and T. M. Fredericka. 2011. "INFOhio's 21st Century Learning Commons: Transforming How Educators Use and Think about School Libraries." *Teacher Librarian* 38 (5): 21–26.

Small, R. V. et al. 2009. "Reading Incentives that Work: No-Cost Strategies to Motivate Kids to Read and Love It!" *School Library Monthly* 25 (9): 27–31.

Warlick, D. 2005. "Building Web Sites That Work for Your Media Center." *Knowledge Quest* 33 (3): 13–15.

APPENDIX D: Additional Suggested Reading

CONTINUED FROM PAGE 86

2.7 BUILDING THE LEARNING ENVIRONMENT: Outreach

Coatney, S. 2009. "Learning to Lead…" *School Library Monthly* 26 (2): 41–43.

Corey, L. 2002. "The Role of the Library Media Specialist in Standards-Based Learning." *Knowledge Quest* 31 (2): 21–23.

Davis, S. 2004. "Harnessing the Power of Parent Volunteers: Starting a Friends of the Library Group at Your School." *Knowledge Quest* 33 (1): 30–31.

DelGuidice, M., and R. Luna. 2012. *Make a Big Impact @Your School Board Meeting.* Santa Barbara, CA: Linworth.

Fontichiaro, K. 2011. "Creating eReader Content." *School Library Monthly* 28 (2): 26.

Fredrick, K. 2011. "Assessment for Program Growth: Thinking about Practice." *School Library Monthly* 28 (3): 23–25.

Hartzell, G. 2007. "How Do Decision-Makers Become Library Media Advocates?" *Knowledge Quest* 36 (1): 32–35.

Harvey, C. A., II. 2007. "Connecting the Library Media Center and Parents." *School Library Media Activities Monthly* 23 (6): 25–27.

———. 2012. "The New Boss!" *School Library Monthly* 28 (5): 13–15.

Jensen, A. 2008. "Presenting the Evidence: Librarian's Annual Report to the Principal." *Knowledge Quest* 37 (2): 28–32.

Johns, S. K. 2007. "Advocacy: AASL Puts the Puzzle Together." *Knowledge Quest* 36 (1): 4–7.

———. 2008. "AASL and Parents: A Partnership for Power." *Knowledge Quest* 36 (3): 4–6.

Kerby, M. 2010. "How One School Librarian Became an Author." *Library Media Connection* 28 (6): 10–13.

Kerr, E. 2011. "Engaging the Decision-Makers and the Influencers." *Teacher Librarian* 38 (3): 69–71.

Kowalski, S. 2011. "Reach Out, Make Connections, Thrive." *Teacher Librarian* 38 (5): 67–68.

Lerch, M. T., and J. Welch. 2004. *Serving Homeschooled Teens and Their Parents.* Westport, CT: Libraries Unlimited.

Library Research Service. 2012. "School Library Information." <www.lrs.org/school> (accessed March 14, 2012).

McGahey, M. 2005. "Hosting a Family Literacy Night at Your School." *Teacher Librarian* 32 (5): 28–30.

Oakleaf, M., and P. L. Owen. 2010. "Closing the 12–13 Gap Together: School and College Librarians Supporting 21st Century Learners." *Teacher Librarian* 37 (4): 52–58.

Partnership for 21st Century Skills. 2009. "2009 MILE Guide: Milestones for Improving Learning & Education." <www.p21.org/index.php?option=com_content&view=article&id=800&Itemid=52> (June 10, 2012).

———. 2011. "Tools & Resources: P21 Common Core Toolkit." <www.p21.org/tools-and-resources/publications/p21-common-core-toolkit> (accessed March 14, 2012).

Patrick, G. D. 2012. "Grass Roots Advocacy." *School Library Monthly* 28 (5): 30–32.

Pipkin, A. M. 2009. "Working with Parents to Achieve National Board Certification." *Library Media Connection* 27 (5): 24–25.

Staino, R. 2007. "Friends Groups: Finding Their Way into Library Media Centers." *School Library Media Activities Monthly* 24 (3): 43–45.

Tannetta, M. 2006. "Internet Safety Night Brought to You by the Library Media Specialist." *School Library Media Activities Monthly* 23 (2): 31–32.

Kent State University Libraries. "TRAILS: Tool for Real-Time Assessment of Information Literacy Skills." 2012. <www.trails-9.org> (accessed March 14, 2012).

Kent State University. "Transitioning to College: Helping You Succeed." 2012. <www. transitioning2college.org> (accessed March 14, 2012).

Van Dusen, M. 2007. "Open Up with Community Outreach." *Library Media Connection* 25 (6): 24–26.

Young, T. 2010. "Marketing Your School Library Media Center: What We Can Learn from National Bookstores." *Library Media Connection* 28 (6): 18–20.

CONTINUED FROM PAGE 93

2.8 BUILDING THE LEARNING ENVIRONMENT: Professional Development

Fredrick, K. 2011. "Weaving Your Virtual Seminar: Create a Webinar." *School Library Monthly* 27 (5): 39–41.

Harlan, M. A. 2009. *Personal Learning Networks: Professional Development for the Isolated School Librarian.* Westport, CT: Libraries Unlimited.

Johns, S. J. et al. 2010. "Pass It Forward: Teaching as an Adjunct." *Knowledge Quest* 38 (5): 40–45.

Schwelik, J. C., and T. M. Fredericka. 2011. "INFOhio's 21st Century Learning Commons: Transforming How Educators Use and Think about School Libraries." *Teacher Librarian* 38 (5): 21–26.

Stephens, W. S. 2011. "The School Librarian as Leader: Out of the Middle, Into the Foreground." *Knowledge Quest* 39 (5): 18–21.

Young, T. E., and C. A. Harvey II. 2010. "Professional Development on a Shoestring." *School Library Monthly* 26 (9): 18–21.

Yucht, A. 2009. "Building Your Personal Learning Network." *Information Searcher* 19 (1): 11–14.

———. 2011. "Conference-Going Strategies, Redux." *Knowledge Quest* 39 (5): 64–67.

APPENDIX D: Additional Suggested Reading

CONTINUED FROM PAGE 98

3.1 EMPOWERING LEARNING THROUGH LEADERSHIP: Leadership

Helvering, D. et al. 2010. "District Leadership and Administration." *Knowledge Quest* 38 (5): 22–25.

International Society for Technology in Education. "ISTE NETS: The Standards for Learning, Leading, and Teaching in the Digital Age." <www.iste.org/standards.aspx> (accessed March 16, 2012).

Jaeger, P. 2012. "We Don't Live in A Multiple-Choice World: Inquiry and the Common Core." *Library Media Connection* 30 (4): 10–12.

Johns, S. K. 2011. "School Librarians Taking the Leadership Challenge." *School Library Monthly* 27 (4): 37–39.

Kramer, P. K. 2011. "Common Core and School Librarians: An Interview with Joyce Karon." *School Library Monthly* 28 (1): 8–10.

Levitov, D., S. Coatney, J. Di Giambattista, and B. Woolls. 2010. "New Directions: The Unplanned Path to Publishing." *Knowledge Quest* 38 (5): 46–51.

Martin, A. M. 2012. *Seven Steps to an Award Winning School Library Program*, 2nd ed. Santa Barbara, CA: Libraries Unlimited.

Miller, S. J. 1999. "Professional Development for the Library Media Specialist." *Book Report* 17 (5): 20–21.

National Board for Professional Teaching Standards. 2007. *NBPTS Library Media Standards for Teachers of Students Ages 3–18+.* <www.nbpts.org/userfiles/File/ecya_lm_standards.pdf> (accessed March 7, 2012).

Sheldon, B. E. 2010. *Interpersonal Skills, Theory, and Practice: The Librarian's Guide to Becoming a Leader.* Santa Barbara, CA: Libaries Unlimited.

Todd, R. J. 2008. "A Question of Evidence." *Knowledge Quest* 37 (2): 16–21.

Trinkle, C. 2009. "Twitter as a Professional Learning Community." *School Library Monthly* 26 (4): 22–23.

U.S. Department of Education. 2012. "Race to the Top Fund." <www2.ed.gov/programs/racetothetop/index.html> (accessed June 10, 2012).

Walsh, A., and P. Inala. 2010. *Active Learning Techniques: Practical Examples.* Oxford, UK: Chandos.

Williamson, K., A. Archibald, and J. McGregor. 2010. "Shared Vision: A Key to Successful Collaboration?" *School Libraries Worldwide* 16 (2): 16–30.

Zmuda, A., and V. H. Harada. 2008. "Librarians as Learning Specialists: Moving from the Margins to the Mainstream of School Leadership." *Teacher Librarian* 36 (1): 15–20.

APPENDIX D: Additional Suggested Reading

My Additonal Suggested Reading Notes

_____

_____

_____

_____

_____

_____

_____

_____

_____

_____

_____

_____

_____

_____

_____

_____

_____

_____

_____

_____

_____

_____

_____

_____

_____

APPENDIX E:
Works Cited

American Association of School Librarians. 2007. "Standards for the 21st-Century Learner." <http://ala.org/ala/mgrps/divs/aasl/guidelinesandstandards/learningstandards/AASL_LearningStandards.pdf> (accessed May 8, 2011).

———. 2009. *Empowering Learners: Guidelines for School Library Programs.* Chicago: ALA.

———. 2009. *Standards for the 21st-Century Learner in Action.* Chicago: AASL.

———. 2010. *A Planning Guide for Empowering Learners with School Library Program Assessment Rubric.* Chicago: AASL.

Common Core State Standards Initiative. 2011a. "About the Standards." <http://corestandards.org/about-the-standards> (accessed May 10, 2012).

———. 2011b. "Process." <http://corestandards.org/about-the-standards/process> (accessed May 10, 2012).

Owen, Patricia L. 2011. "An Improved 'Form of Our Own': A 21st Century Approach to School Librarian Evaluation." *Library Media Connection.* 30-33.

U.S. Department of Education. 2009. "Race To The Top Program Executive Summary." <http://www2.ed.gov/programs/racetothetop/executive-summary.pdf> (accessed May 15, 2012).

My Notes

_____

_____

_____

_____

_____

_____

_____

_____

_____

_____

_____

_____

_____

_____

_____

APPENDIX F:
My Action Plan Template

ACTION _____

_____

_____

MY GOAL	Goal Type
	☐ Short-term
	☐ Long-term
	☐ Part of Strategic Plan
	☐ Professional Development
	☐ Leader Role
	☐ Instructional Partner Role
	☐ Info. Specialist Role
	☐ Teacher Role
	☐ Program Admin.Role

My Target Audience

SCHOOL COMMUNITY:
☐ Students
☐ Teachers
☐ Administrators
☐ Advisory Committee
☐ Planning Committee
☐ Friends of the Library
☐ Volunteers (Student/Adult)

EXTERNAL STAKEHOLDERS:
☐ Parents
☐ Local Community
☐ Business Community
☐ Public Library
☐ Academic Library
☐ State Community
☐ National Community
☐ Global Community

TASK 1		TASK 2	
	TIMELINE		**TIMELINE**
	☐ This Week		☐ This Week
	☐ This Month		☐ This Month
	☐ This Grading Period		☐ This Grading Period
	☐ This Semester		☐ This Semester
	☐ This Year		☐ This Year
	☐ Next Year		☐ Next Year
	☐ 2–3 Year Plan		☐ 2–3 Year Plan

MY PROFESSIONAL DEVELOPMENT PLANS

VENUE

☐ District In-Service
☐ Local/Regional Conference
☐ State Conference
☐ AASL National Conference
☐ Community Learning
☐ College Course
☐ Evidence Collection
☐ Action Research
☐ Readings